THE COMPLETE LETTER-WRITER FOR LADIES AND GENTLEMEN

THE COMPLETE LETTER-WRITER FOR LADIES AND GENTLEMEN

Containing
Specimen Letters
on a variety of subjects including

INVITATIONS	BUSINESS
INTRODUCTIONS	EMPLOYMENT
CONGRATULATION	RENT AND BILLS
CONDOLENCE	MARRIAGE

etc.

WARD, LOCK & CO., LIMITED

London, Melbourne and Johannesburg

1235

MADE IN ENGLAND

Printed in Great Britain by A. Quick & Co. Ltd., Clacton-on-Sea, Essex

CONTENTS

LADIES' CORRESPONDENCE

Invitations

Announcements and Letters of Congratulation and Condolence

Requests

Engagement and Marriage

Business

Employment

Shipping and Export

GENTLEMEN'S CORRESPONDENCE

Invitations

1. Invitation to Dinner.
2. Reply to above.
3. Another reply, declining.
4. Invitation, less formal.
5. Reply to above.
6. Another reply, declining.
7. Invitation to lunch at a Restaurant.
8. Reply accepting.
9. Reply declining.
10. Invitation to a Lady to Lunch.
11. Formal Invitation to a Wedding.
12. Acceptance.
13. Declining above.
14. Formal Invitation to an At Home.
15. Acceptance of above.
16. Formal Invitations to Dances, Bridge Parties, Garden Parties and Similar Functions.
17. Invitation to Official Function.
18. Acceptance of above.
19. Letter of Thanks for an Evening's Entertainment.
20. Invitation to Stay.
21. Reply to above.
22. Another, declining.
23. Letter of Thanks for a Visit.
24. Invitation to go on a Motor Tour.

Announcements, Letters of Congratulation and Condolence

Requests, with Replies

Engagement and Marriage

Business

Inquiries and References

Landlord and Tenant

Miscellaneous Business

From Parents, To and About their Children

Preface

The arrangement of this book calls for no elaborate explanation. There are two comprehensive sections, one for Ladies and the other for Gentlemen, each containing letters which, with a little adaptation, can be used for almost all occasions involving personal, social and business matters.

It is not intended that the letters set out here should be copied word for word. These letters are drafts, to be used as a guide to form and content, and indicating the type of letter that is appropriate for a variety of occasions.

In addition to a wide range of model letters, THE COMPLETE LETTER-WRITER FOR LADIES AND GENTLEMEN contains a section on the writing and composition of letters, with information about the choice of writing materials and other useful advice, and precise instruction as to the forms to be observed in addressing people of rank and standing—a matter upon which even the socially expert often display ignorance.

THE EDITOR

Warwick House,
116 Baker Street,
London, W.1.

FORMS OF ADDRESS FOR THE COMMENCEMENT AND CONCLUSION OF LETTERS

The Sovereign.
Address: To The Queen's Most Excellent Majesty.
Begin: Your Majesty; Madam; *or* May it please Your Majesty.
End: I have the honour to be, Your Majesty's most obedient subject and servant.

The Duke of Edinburgh.
Address: To His Royal Highness the Duke of Edinburgh.
Begin: Your Royal Highness; *or* Sir.
End: I have the honour to be, Your Royal Highness' most obedient servant.

The Queen Mother.
Address: To Her Majesty Queen Elizabeth the Queen Mother.
Begin: Your Majesty; Madam; *or* May it please Your Majesty.
End: I have the honour to be, Your Majesty's most obedient servant.

The Prince of Wales.
Address: To His Royal Highness the Prince of Wales.
Begin: Your Royal Highness; *or* Sir.
End: I have the honour to be, Your Royal Highness' most obedient servant.

Royal Princes and Dukes. As for H.R.H. the Duke of Edinburgh.

Royal Princesses and Duchesses.
Address: To Her Royal Highness the Princess Anne *or* To Her Royal Highness the Duchess of Kent.

Begin: Your Royal Highness; *or* Madam.
End: I have the honour to be, Your Royal Highness' most obedient servant.

A Duke or Duchess.
Address: To His Grace the Duke of Barsetshire (or, Her Grace, the Duchess of Barsetshire).
Begin: My Lord Duke *or* Sir *or* Your Grace *or* Madam.
End: I have the honour to be, Your Grace's most obedient servant. The informal beginning and ending is "Dear Duke" or "Dear Duchess" and "Yours sincerely."

Duke's Children. The eldest son of a duke ranks as a peer by courtesy and is addressed as a Marquis or an Earl as the case may be, his sons being addressed as peer's sons.

Younger Sons of a Duke.
Address: The Lord John Plantagenet.
Begin: My Lord; *or*, informally, Dear Lord John.
End: Your Lordship's most obedient servant; informally, Yours sincerely.

The Wife of a Duke's Younger Son.
Address: The Lady John Plantagenet.
Begin: My Lady; or Dear Lady John.
End: Your Ladyship's most obedient servant; or, Yours sincerely.

Duke's Daughters (if unmarried).
Address: The Lady Maud Millington-Foster.
Begin: Madam; or Dear Lady Maud.
End: Your Ladyship's most obedient servant; or, Yours sincerely.
N.B. If a Duke's daughter marries a Peer she assumes his rank and is addressed as a countess, etc. If she marries a commoner, she continues to be addressed as the daughter of a duke, changing only her surname. For family surnames of the members of the peerage, see Whitaker's Almanac.

Marquis or Marchioness.
Address: To the Most Honourable the Marquis (or Marchioness) of Steyne.
Begin: My Lord Marquis, or Sir, or Dear Lord Steyne; or Madam, or Dear Lady Steyne.
End: Your Lordship's (or, Your Ladyship's) most obedient servant; or, Yours sincerely.

Children of a Marquis. The oldest son of a Marquis takes his father's second title, and is addressed as a peer, his wife and children as a peer's wife and children. Younger sons, and daughters, of a Marquis, are given the title Lord or Lady as for the children of dukes.

Earl or Countess.
Address: To the Right Hon. the Earl (or Countess) of Camberley.
Begin: My Lord or Sir; My Lady or Madam; or, informally, Dear Lord Camberley or Dear Lady Camberley.
End: Your Lordship's (or, Ladyship's) most obedient servant. Or, Yours sincerely.

Children of an Earl. An Earl's eldest son ranks as a Viscount and is addressed as such. Daughters and younger sons take the title "Honourable" used in place of "Mr." or "Miss".
Address: The Hon. Freddy Finch-Fallow. The Hon. Jane Finch-Fallow.

Begin: Dear Sir, or Dear Madam, or Dear Mr. Finch-Fallow or Dear Miss Finch-Fallow.
End: Yours faithfully, or Yours sincerely.
N.B. The daughter of an Earl who marries an untitled man becomes "The Hon. Mrs. Smith". The wife of the son of an earl is "The Hon. Mrs. Freddy Finch-Fallow".

Viscount or Viscountess.
Address: To the Right Honourable the Viscount Milverton; To the Right Honourable the Viscountess Milverton.
Begin: My Lord, Your Ladyship, Sir, or Madam. Informally, Dear Lord Milverton, Dear Lady Milverton.
End: Your Lordship's (Ladyship's) obedient Servant. Informally, Yours sincerely.

Children of a Viscount. As for children of an earl.

A Baron or Baroness.
Address: To the Right Honourable the Lord Annesley; To the Right Honourable the Lady Annesley, or Baroness Annesley.
Begin and *End:* As for Viscount and Viscountess.

A Baroness in her own right is addressed similarly to a lady who is the wife of a baron, and her children as a baron's children.

Widows of peers retain their title of "Duchess", "Countess", etc., so long as the next peer remains unmarried, after which they become "The Dowager Duchess of Barsetshire". "The Dowager Marchioness of Mercia", etc., if the mother or grandmother of the new peer. If not so related to the new peer, the widow usually takes the title "Mary, Duchess of Barsetshire", "Anne, Marchioness of Mercia", etc. Beginnings and endings of letters, as for wives of peers.

Baronets and Knights and their Wives.
Address: To Sir Norman Campbell, Bart. (or, Bt.); To Lady Campbell. To Sir Sidney Waterlow; To Lady Waterlow.
Begin: Sir; Dear Sir Norman; Dear Lady Campbell; Dear Sir Sidney; Dear Lady Waterlow; Madam.
End: Your obedient servant; Yours faithfully; Yours sincerely.

Widows of Baronets become either The Dowager Lady Campbell or Lavinia, Lady Campbell, following the same rule as for widows of peers (q.v.). Letters to them begin and end in the same way as when their husbands were alive. Widows of knights continue to be addressed in the same way as when their husbands were alive.

Dames.
Address: Dame Margaret Ferguson; *or*, Miss Margaret Ferguson, D.B.E.

Begin: Dear Dame Margaret; or, Madam.
End: Yours faithfully; Yours sincerely.

Children of Life Peers and Peeresses are addressed as private persons.

Private Persons.
Address: James Smith, Esq.
Begin: Dear Sir; or, Dear Mr. Smith.
End: Yours faithfully; Yours sincerely; Yours truly.
N.B. Although strictly speaking Esquire is a title to which only certain people have the right (e.g., landed gentry, members of the bar, etc.) its use for all private gentlemen as a matter of courtesy is sanctioned by modern custom, both in business and private correspondence.

Ladies.
Address: Mrs. James Smith or Mrs. J. Smith; Miss Smith (if the eldest unmarried daughter); Miss Pamela Smith or Miss P. Smith if a younger unmarried daughter.
Begin: Dear Mrs. Smith, Dear Miss Smith.
End: Yours faithfully; Yours sincerely; Yours truly.
N.B. The form "Mrs. Margaret Smith" or "Mrs. M. Smith" is used chiefly for divorcees and sometimes for women who have a business career in their own right. Otherwise it is best avoided.
Where two ladies have the same name, e.g., a mother-in-law and daughter-in-law who may both be Mrs. James Smith, the younger may be addressed as Mrs. James Smith, Jun. It is incorrect to address the older as Mrs. James Smith, Sen.

Government and Other Officials.
The Prime Minister.
Address: The Right Hon. Alfred Winston, P.C., M.P., Prime Minister.
Begin: Dear Mr. Prime Minister; Dear Mr. Winston; Dear Sir Alfred (if a knight); Dear Prime Minister (informal).
End: Yours faithfully; Yours sincerely.

Prime Ministers of Commonwealth Countries.
Address: The Right Hon. John MacIlwray, P.C., M.P., Prime Minister of New Zealand.
Begin and *End* as for the British Prime Minister.

Members of the British Cabinet.
Address: The Right Hon. Edward Cardwell, P.C., M.P., Secretary of——.
Begin: Dear Mr. Secretary; Dear Mr. Cardwell.
End: Yours faithfully; Yours sincerely.

If a Woman:
Address: The Right Hon. Ellen Bondfield, P.C., M.P., Minister of Education.

Begin: Dear Madam Minister; Dear Miss (or Mrs.).
End: Yours faithfully; Yours sincerely.

The Speaker of the House of Commons.
Address: To the Right Hon. James Fotherington, Speaker of the House of Commons.
Begin: Sir; Dear Mr. Speaker.
End: Your obedient servant; Yours faithfully; Yours sincerely.

Privy Councillors. All Privy Councillors, other than Dukes and Marquesses, have the title Right Honourable. In practice this is used, in correspondence, only in addressing those who have no other title.
Address: The Right Hon. Peter Smith, P.C.; The Right Hon. Edith Brown, P.C.
Begin: Dear Sir; Dear Mr. Smith; Dear Madam; Madam; Dear Miss Brown.
End: Yours faithfully; Yours sincerely.

Member of Parliament. If titled, address according to rank; begin and end letter accordingly. If untitled, address as a private person, with the addition of the letters M.P. after the address. Beginning and end of letter, as for private person.

Governor-General of a Dominion or Colony.
Address: To His Excellency Sir Edward Jones, Governor-General of Australia. (Or, Lord Jones, or according to rank.)
Begin: Your Excellency; Dear Governor-General; Dear Sir Edward (or, Dear Lord Jones).
End: Your Excellency's obedient servant; Yours faithfully; Yours sincerely.

Ambassadors.
Address: To His Excellency the Right Hon. Michael Murdoch (or, The Earl of Murdoch, etc., according to rank); Her Britannic Majesty's Ambassador.
Begin: Your Excellency; Sir; Dear Lord Murdoch (or, according to rank).
End: Your Excellency's obedient servant; Yours faithfully; Yours sincerely.

Ministers, Envoys, Consuls, Legation Secretaries.
Address: Henry Brown, Esq. (or according to rank); Her Britannic Majesty's Minister (or, Consul, or, Secretary to the Legation).
Begin and *End:* As for private individuals or according to rank.

Commonwealth Privy Councillors. As Privy Councillors of Great Britain, except that the title is "The Honourable", not "The Right Honourable".

The Wives of the Above Officials are addressed according to their private rank, *not* with reference to their husband's official position.

Clergymen.

Archbishop.

Address: To His Grace the Lord Archbishop of Canterbury.

Begin: My Lord Archbishop; Your Grace; Dear Lord Archbishop (informal).

End: Your Lordship's obedient servant; Yours respectfully; Yours sincerely.

Bishops.

Address: To the Right Reverend the Lord Bishop of Barchester.

Begin: My Lord Bishop; Dear Bishop (informal).

End: Your most obedient servant; Yours faithfully; Yours sincerely.

Roman Catholic Bishops and Archbishops.

Address: His Excellency the Most Reverend Michael O'Flaherty, Archbishop (or Bishop) of ——.

Begin: Your Excellency; Dear Archbishop; Dear Bishop.

End: Your Excellency's Most obedient servant; Yours respectfully; Yours sincerely.

Scottish Bishops are addressed personally as Right Rev. Bishop Mackenzie, D.D.; *not* The Right Rev. the Lord Bishop of Glamis.

Deans and Archdeacons.

Address: To the Very Reverend the Dean of Barchester; To the Venerable the Archdeacon.

Begin: Very Reverend Sir; Dear Dean; Venerable Sir; Dear Archdeacon.

End: Your obedient servant; Yours faithfully; Yours sincerely.

Canon.

Address: The Rev. Canon Browne, D.D.

Begin: Reverend Sir; Dear Canon; Dear Canon Browne.

End: Your obedient servant; Yours faithfully; Yours sincerely.

Clergymen and Ministers, if with a Doctor's degree.

Address: The Rev. James Chasuble, D.D.

Begin: Dear Dr. Chasuble; Dear Rector; Dear Vicar; Dear Sir.

End: Yours faithfully; Yours sincerely.

If without a Doctor's degree.

Address: The Rev. John Phillips, B.A.

Begin: Dear Mr. Phillips; Dear Rector; Dear Vicar; Dear Father Phillips; Dear Sir.

End: Yours faithfully; Yours sincerely.

Jewish Rabbi.

Address: Rabbi Aaron Joseph.

Begin: Dear Rabbi Joseph; Dear Rabbi.

End: Yours faithfully; Yours sincerely.

The Wives of Clergymen are invariably addressed by their private rank, not according to their husband's office. E.g., although a Bishop may be addressed as "My Lord Bishop" his wife will still be addressed as "Dear Mrs. Proudie" or "Dear Madam", unless she happens to have a title in her own right.

Clergymen who have titles of secular rank as well as their church title, are addressed by both, the church title being put first. Thus, the son of a Duke who became a curate would be addressed as The Rev. Lord James Jernigan; the son of an Earl would be The Rev. The Hon. John Morrell. Begin and end letters as for the sons of peers. Their wives are addressed by the secular rank only, Lady James Jernigan or The Hon. Mrs. John Morrell.

Officers of the Services.
Address: with titles according to rank. Admiral Lord Hornblower, K.G.; or General Sir William Everett, K.C.M.G.; Captain, *or* Commander, Hardy, R.N.; Major William Jones, V.C.; Lieutenant Andrews, R.N.; Group Captain T. Shaw, R.A.F.
It is usual to add after the officer's name either the letters R.N. or R.A.F., or, if in the army, the initials or name of his regiment, e.g., R.A. or R.A.S.C.; these initials come *before* any decorations or distinctions such as V.C., D.S.O., etc.
Begin: Sir; Dear Captain Andrews.
End: I am, sir, your obedient servant; Yours faithfully; Yours sincerely.

Wives of Officers are addressed by their private rank; e.g., an Admiral's wife will be Mrs. Hornblower, unless she has rank of her own, e.g., Lady Barbara Hornblower.

The Medical Profession.
Address: Dr. S. Palmer or S. Palmer, Esq., M.D.
Begin: Dear Sir; Dear Dr. Palmer.
End: Yours faithfully; Yours sincerely.
N.B. Surgeons are addressed as Mr. *not* Dr.

The Lord Chancellor.
Address: To The Right Honourable the Lord High Chancellor of England.
Begin: My Lord Chancellor; My Lord; Dear Lord Whigham (informal).
End: Your Lordship's obedient servant; Yours sincerely.

Lord Chief Justice.
Address: To the Right Honourable the Lord Chief Justice of England; or To the Right Honourable Lord Burkhill, Lord Chief Justice of England (according to rank).
Begin: My Lord; Sir; Dear Lord Burkhall.
End: Your Lordship's obedient servant; Yours sincerely.

The Lord Advocate.
Address: To the Right Honourable the Lord Advocate; *or* To the Right Honourable James Burns, Lord Advocate.
Begin: Sir; Dear Lord Advocate.
End: Your obedient Servant; Yours faithfully; Yours sincerely.

Lord Justice of Appeal.
Address: To the Right Hon. Lord Justice Simpson.
Begin: My Lord; Sir; Dear Lord Simpson *or* Dear Sir John (according to rank).
End: Your obedient servant; Yours faithfully; Yours sincerely.

High Court Judge.
Address: To the Honourable Mr. Justice Benson.
Begin: Sir; Dear Sir; Dear Mr. Justice Benson.
End: Your obedient servant; Yours faithfully; Yours sincerely.

County Court Judge.
Address: To His Honour Judge Warner.
Begin: Your Honour; Sir; Dear Judge Warner.
End: As for High Court Judge.

Lord Mayor.
Address: The Right Honourable the Lord Mayor of Barchester; *or* The Right Hon. Sir Arthur Beecham, Lord Mayor of Barchester.
Begin and *End:* as for a Baron.

Mayor.
Address: The Worshipful the Mayor of Silchester.
Begin: Your Worship; Sir; Dear Mr. Mayor.
End: Yours faithfully; Yours sincerely.

The Wife of a Mayor or Lord Mayor is the Mayoress or Lady Mayoress. She is not addressed as "Right Honourable" or "Worshipful". Letters to her begin "Madam", "Dear Lady Mayoress" or "Dear Madam Mayoress" and end as for the Mayor.

A Woman Mayor is addressed exactly as a man Mayor. Letters to her begin "Madam", "Your Worship", "Dear Madam Mayor" or, occasionally, "Dear Mr. Mayor". *Never* use the word "Mayoress" for a woman Mayor.

The Art of Letter-Writing

It is a paradox of modern life that the art of letter-writing has declined at just the same time as a good education has become freely available to all. To a great extent this can be blamed upon the ease of modern communications. Except during periods of prolonged separation, most of us neglect to write long or full letters; it is so much easier to pick up a telephone or use the car or motor scooter for a personal meeting and chat.

Even when a written letter really seems called for, when one is sending congratulations upon some happy occasion, or wants to convey sympathy to a bereaved friend—many people, alas, mistrust their powers of composition and prefer to rely upon a card bought from the stationer. More's the pity, for a letter over which the writer has taken some thought and trouble and which therefore bears the stamp of her own personality, is a thousand times more worth having than a mass produced greeting bought ready made.

Then there are occasions when one has a business letter to write and has, perhaps, no training in business procedure. Letters of introduction, letters asking a favour, letters of inquiry about hotel accommodation, all these have a distinct form of their own, knowledge of which stamps the writer as a person of intelligence, education and discrimination.

In the following pages we give a selection of typical letters which can be modified to meet a wide variety of circumstances. It is not suggested that the examples given should be copied literally; they are intended to serve as a guide, but almost always in a specific situation there will be small modifications which common sense will suggest, which will give a letter a more personal touch.

There are certain points which should always be observed in correspondence.

Address and Date. The address from which one is writing, and the date, should be written, clearly and in full, at the top of any letter. The only possible exception is, that in writing to a close friend who will know one's address, this may be omitted; the date should always be given. Even if you are saying nothing more important than "it rained here yesterday", the recipient will like to know when "yesterday" was; and undated letters are the bane of the biographer!

If a reply is expected on a matter of business or semi-business, from someone one does not correspond with regularly, it is courteous to enclose a stamped addressed envelope for the reply, but this does not take the place of the address at the top of the letter, which must still be given.

If one is expecting to write many business letters, it is best to have printed headings on the writing paper giving the address and leaving only the date to be filled in. Printed or engraved writing paper also lends elegance to private correspondence, but is by no means obligatory. Most good printing firms can show examples of the kind of thing that is usual; in choosing a style, whether for business or private letters, simplicity is in the best taste.

Business letters which are typed should always be signed in ink by the writers. The custom is also growing of writing the beginning of the letter "Dear Mr. Jones" or "Dear Miss Smith" by hand. The use of the typewriter for personal correspondence is sanctioned by modern usage, but it is better to write by hand if one has the faintest suspicion that the recipient might feel a typewritten letter discourteous.

Choice of paper and ink. White, grey, cream and very pale blue are the only colours which are invariably correct and in good taste for writing paper, although other pale pastel shades are sometimes permissible for very personal correspondence. Ink should be blue, black, or blue-black; coloured inks are not considered in good taste. When possible, the size of the paper should be suitable for the length of the letter to be written, so that it may be attractively set out and spaced.

The beginning and ending. All except purely personal letters to friends should have an "address" or "superscription", i.e., the full formal name and title of the person being written to. For example: To the Right Honourable the Earl of Clanricarde, Clanricarde Castle, Berkshire; or, To the Editor of the *Times*, Printing House Square, London, E.C.4. This "superscription" is set out *either* at the top left hand of the letter, *or* at the bottom and to the left. Full forms of address for various personages will be found in the section following the list of Contents.

Business letters to strangers usually begin, after the appropriate superscription, with "Dear Sir" or "Dear Madam" but if one knows the recipient or has spoken to them on the telephone, it is usual to begin "Dear Mr. Jones", "Dear Miss Jenkins" and so forth. In many firms nowadays Christian names are increasingly used and it is quite permissible to write "Dear Jane" to a business acquaintance with whom one is on Christian name terms, unless the custom of the firm is against it. "Dear Jane Jenkins" is best avoided.

Some firms prefer that letters are not addressed to individuals by name; in this case, begin "Dear Sirs" and be careful to quote any reference numbers used by the firm, to ensure that it reaches the person or department dealing with the matter.

"My dear Jane", "My dear Mrs. Jones" and so on are seldom used in Great Britain except between very close friends who would usually be on Christian name terms. In America the usage is different—there "Dear Mrs. Jones" indicates greater intimacy, "My dear Mrs. Jones" is the way comparative strangers are addressed.

The endings of letters vary according to the way in which the letter has begun. The usual custom with formal or business letters is to end "Yours faithfully" if the letter has begun "Dear Sir" or "Dear Madam"; "Yours sincerely" if it has begun "Dear Miss Smith" or "Dear Mr. Brown"; and either "Yours sincerely" or just "Yours" if it has begun with the Christian name of the recipient. The same applies to letters on semi-business matters to people one does not know well.

Naturally, if one is on Christian name terms with a countess, it is quite in order to begin a letter to her, "Dear Dorothy" and end "Yours ever, Joan". Friends are friends, and are written to as such, whatever their rank, but it is important not to seem to presume upon slighter acquaintance.

When writing informally to friends and acquaintances, "Yours sincerely", "Yours always", "Yours as ever", "Yours affectionately", or just "Yours" are all quite correct, and one's choice will depend upon the degree of friendship and other circumstances. "Yours with love" or "With love from" are usually kept for relations and very close friends.

Many women find it difficult to know whether they should put "Miss" or "Mrs." either as part of their signature or in brackets before, after, or underneath. Strictly speaking, an unmarried woman should not put any title but simply sign herself "Jane Wilkins", and it is then supposed to be assumed that she is addressed as "Miss" in the reply. A married woman signs similarly "Belinda Brown" but either encloses her card which will give her name as "Mrs. John Brown" or alternatively inscribes the words "Mrs. John Brown" *at the bottom left hand corner* of the letter.

Since, however, many people may be unaware of this rule of etiquette, it is often kinder and more thoughtful to give some indication, especially if a reply is expected. If one wants to do this, to write "Miss Jane Wilkins" in the bottom left hand corner of the letter, quite separately from the signature, is the best way of conveying the information.

The impersonal style, e.g., "Mrs. Jones presents her compliments to Mrs. Smith and will feel obliged if she will be so good as to return the book, etc., etc." is no longer necessary on *any* occasion except for formal invitations and replies to them.

What to say. Except for social letters to friends, when news, comment, description and any other remarks may be included, one should always write as briefly as possible and keep strictly to the point. In a business letter, only business matters should be mentioned, although it is permissible, when writing to someone with whom one is on friendly terms, to include some very brief personal message such as "I hope you had a good holiday" or "Trusting you are now fully recovered from influenza". On the whole, however, if social letters are to be written to business people it is more polite to send them to the private address, or at the least, put them in a separate envelope, marked "private".

The best way to judge what to include and what to leave out is to imagine oneself for a moment in the place of the recipient. For instance, one's bank manager may be an old friend or relative whom one has known as "Tubby" ever since school days, but as business letters are usually opened by a secretary and preserved in the files, it would be highly tactless to begin a letter to him "Dear Tubby"! Similarly, if one is inviting a friend to stay, a moment's reflection will show that she will like to be told what the programme will be, so that she can decide what clothes to bring. Any letter which will be followed by action of any kind, e.g., arranging a meeting, sending an order to a shop, inviting a friend to dine, should include all details necessary for action: full information about time and place of meeting; the exact size, colour and style of article required from the shop; date and time of the dinner party and perhaps a note of the route to enable your friend to reach your house with the minimum of trouble. Imagination, and putting oneself in the recipient's shoes, will show just what is needed.

Putting oneself in the recipient's place should also show (much more often than it actually does) the importance of a clear and legible signature. A firm, clear, *readable* signature can show real character and make a valuable first impression upon a total stranger.

Quite as important as what to say, is what to leave out. Would-be humourous remarks are often misinterpreted when made in a letter, without the twinkle in the eye or the hint of a smile which, in conversation, would show that a joke is intended. Extreme frankness can be hurtful, and a comment that, spoken, would quickly pass over, can, if committed to writing, be kept and brooded upon, often to the real detriment of friendship. Actual rudeness, or ill-natured remarks about a third party should (it need hardly be said) never be put in writing. "If in doubt, leave it out" is a sound rule in letter writing.

Do not try to impress people in your letters, and never apologise for them. "Forgive my typing this but I am in a hurry" is the kind of thing best left unsaid; if what you are doing really needs apologising for, do not do it!

Although prompt replies should be sent to all correspondence (except for the purely friendly letters which do not call for an urgent answer), letters should not be written in a hurry. Ideally, one should sit down with enough time for careful marshalling of one's thoughts and neat, careful, attractive handwriting, implying unhurried consideration.

Composition and punctuation. Mastery of these two subjects is important; an easy, flowing, simple literary style, with correct use of stops, hyphens, commas, and colons, is the thing to aim at. Good style comes from two things: firstly and much the most important, clarity of thought about what one wants to say, and secondly, acquaintance with the works of the best writers.

Cobbett, Swift and Defoe are supreme among the older

writers for clear forceful style, and of the moderns, Somerset Maugham. The letters of Jane Austen and Charles Lamb are also worth reading. Needless to say, one should not attempt actually to copy anyone else's literary manner; style is an individual thing, and any affectation easily detectable. But study of the great writers gradually and almost unconsciously improves one's own handling of words.

"Fowler's Modern English Usage" is a useful work of reference which is still the best guide both to the niceties of style and pitfalls to be avoided and also to the correct use of punctuation.

It is not necessary always to write in the same style. Absolute correctness and some formality is usual in letters to strangers, or on business; but for personal correspondence, letters to friends, and so forth, a more intimate, natural and friendly style is best. Here again, it is a matter of, firstly, being oneself, and secondly, imagining how things will strike the recipient. This is, indeed, the key to success in all letter-writing.

LETTER-WRITER FOR LADIES

LETTER-WRITER FOR LADIES

INVITATIONS

No. 1—Invitation to Dine

Mr. and Mrs. Smith request the pleasure of the company of Mr. and Mrs. Williams at dinner on Wednesday, October 16th, at 7.30 o'clock for 8 o'clock.

600 King's Road, S.W.3.
Monday, 31st September.

No. 2—Accepting

Mr. and Mrs. Williams thank Mr. and Mrs. Smith for their kind invitation to dine on Wednesday, October 16th, and have much pleasure in accepting.

100 Grove Road, N.W.6.
Wednesday, October 2nd.

No. 3—Invitation

Mr. and Mrs. Munro request the pleasure of the company of Mr. and Mrs. Anderson and of Miss Janet Anderson, at dinner on Wednesday, October 16th at half past seven o'clock.

The Warren,
Bickley.
Monday, September 31st.

No. 4—Reply

Mr. and Mrs. Anderson accept with pleasure Mr. and Mrs. Munro's kind invitation to dinner on Wednesday, 16th October. Miss Janet Anderson regrets that she will be unable to accompany them, owing to a prior engagement.

17 Coke Villas, N.W.3.
Monday, September 31st.

No. 5—Another Reply

Mr. and Mrs. Anderson regret that, owing to a prior engagement, they and their daughter are unable to accept Mr. and Mrs. Munro's kind invitation for Wednesday, 16th October.

17 Coke Villas, N.W.3.
Monday, September 31st.

No. 6—Less Formal Invitation

9 Enfield Villas,
Hornsey, N.8.
Monday, 12th June

Dear Mrs. Johnstone,

Will you give us the pleasure of your company at dinner on Thursday next at half past seven?

Yours sincerely,
Maud Jennings.

No. 7—Reply

Holly House,
Hendon Way, N.W.3.
Tuesday, 13th June

Dear Mrs. Jennings,

Thank you so much for the invitation.

I shall be very pleased to dine with you on Thursday next.

Yours truly,
Edith Johnstone.

No. 8—Formal Invitation to a Wedding

Invitations for weddings are always printed or engraved, the name of the recipient being written in; good stationers will show samples of the sort of thing that is usual.

Mr. and Mrs. Henry Sherwood
request the pleasure of the company of
Mr. and Mrs. John Thompson
on the occasion of
the Marriage of their daughter
Joan Christine
to
Captain Peter Cholmondeley
at St. John's Church, W.1, at 2.30 p.m.
and afterwards at
the Barchester Hotel.

R.S.V.P. to
999 Hyde Park Gardens. W.2.

No. 9—Acceptance

(*Date in full*).

Mr. and Mrs. John Thompson have much pleasure in accepting Mr. and Mrs. Henry Sherwood's kind invitation to the marriage of their daughter Joan Christine on Monday, June 8th.

9 John Street,
Hampstead, N.W.3.

No. 10—Declining above

(*Date in full*).

Mr. and Mrs. John Thompson much regret that they are unable to accept Mr. and Mrs. Sherwood's kind invitation to the marriage of their daughter on June 8th, as they will be out of town.

9 John Street,
Hampstead, N.W.3.

No. 11—Formal Invitation to an At Home

These are usually printed, the name of the recipient being written in. Special cards can be bought from most stationers, with spaces for the filling in of details of time and place. The form is as follows:

Mrs. James Robinson
AT HOME
Monday, June 10th
4 p.m.—6 p.m.

19 John Street,
Hampstead, N.W.3.

R.S.V.P.

No. 12—Acceptance of above

Acceptances or refusals should be formal, as in the case of wedding invitations. For example—

Mrs. Alan Gerrard has much pleasure in accepting the invitation of Mrs. James Robinson for Monday, June 10th at 4 p.m.

11 Dale Road,
N.W.3.

No. 13—Formal Invitations to Dances, Bridge Parties, Garden Parties and similar Entertainments

These follow the form of At Home invitations, the word "Dancing", "Bridge", etc., being added in the left hand bottom corner. The forms of acceptance and refusal are as for wedding invitations.

No. 14—Informal Invitation to a Small Dance

DEAR MRS. JONES,

The girls have persuaded me to arrange a little dance for them during the Christmas holidays, and we plan to have it on Thursday the 17th. Will you and your daughters and your older boy give us the pleasure of your company on that evening at eight o'clock? We should so much like to see your husband also, but I seem to remember he does not care for dancing; still if you can persuade him to come too, we should be so pleased.

Yours sincerely,
HELEN BROWN.

17 Charters Villas,
Bushey.
1st January.

No. 15—Reply

DEAR MRS. BROWN,

It is very kind of you to ask so many of us for the 17th. My daughters and John will be delighted to go, but will you kindly excuse Mr. Jones and myself? Our dancing days are over!

With kind regards,
Yours sincerely,
OLIVIA JONES.

100 Circle Court,
Stanmore.
2nd January.

No. 16—Children's Parties

Invitations for very small children are usually sent on the small illustrated cards to be bought from most stationers. Alternative forms to be written by hand are given below.

DEAR MRS. HUGHES,

I am giving a small party for the twins on Wednesday of next week and we should be so happy if Elizabeth could come. Can you bring her (or, allow your Nanny to bring her) from 3 to 6 o'clock.

Yours sincerely,
MARY MARSTON.

4 The Terrace, N.W.6.

No. 17—Another

(*Date in full*).

DEAR MRS. HUGHES,

I am giving a small party for Jonathan and Simon on Wednesday next, and do hope Elizabeth can come. It is from 3 to 6 o'clock.

Yours sincerely,
MARY MARSTON.

4 The Terrace,
N.W.6.

No. 18—A reply

(*Date in full*).

DEAR MRS. MARSTON,

It is very kind of you to ask Elizabeth to the boys' party and I accept for her with pleasure.

Yours sincerely,
MARION HUGHES.

No. 19—Letter of thanks for an Evening's Entertainment

9 MONTEITH ROW, S.W.3.
(*Date in full*).

DEAR MRS. BARCLAY,

John and I enjoyed ourselves so much at your dinner party last evening. It isn't often these days one has the pleasure of such really sparkling conversation—and I shall long remember your lovely flower arrangements. Altogether a delightful evening; thank you so much.

Yours sincerely,
HELEN HERBERTSON.

No. 20—Invitation to Stay

24 QUEEN'S PARK,
GODALMING.

(*Date in full*).

DEAR ELAINE,

It seems a long time since we saw you and I wonder if you are free to visit us the weekend after next, that is, from the 15th-17th September. The garden is looking nice just now and it would be pleasant if you could come while the fine weather holds. Let me know if I may expect you.

Yours sincerely,
MARGARET BROWN.

No. 21—Reply to above

17 LAKE ROAD,
CANONBURY.

(*Date in full*).

DEAR MRS. BROWN,

Thank you for your letter. It is most kind of you to invite me for the weekend from 15th-17th September and I shall love to come. I will travel down by the train arriving at your station at 11.30 a.m., but please do not trouble to meet the train as I know my way from the station quite well. Please give my love to the children; I am so much looking forward to seeing them again.

Yours sincerely,
ELAINE ROBINSON.

No. 22—Another, declining

17 LAKE ROAD,
CANONBURY.

(*Date in full*).

DEAR MRS. BROWN,

Thank you for your letter and very kind invitation to stay. Unfortunately I am on duty that weekend and shall not be able to get away, which is a great disappointment to me. It would have been so pleasant to see you all again and I would have welcomed the chance to rest and relax in your lovely surroundings.

Please remember me to Mr. Brown and give my love to the children.

Yours sincerely,
ELAINE ROBINSON.

No. 23—Letter of Thanks for a Visit

17 LAKE ROAD,
CANONBURY.

(*Date in full*).

DEAR MRS. BROWN,

I arrived back last evening after quite a quick and pleasant train journey. The carriage never became too crowded and we got in well on time.

I did so much enjoy my stay with you and shall long remember that beautiful drive along the river and the wonderful sunset; it is something to cherish and think about back here in the grimy old city. Thank you very much indeed for my lovely weekend.

Yours very sincerely,
ELAINE ROBINSON.

No. 24.—Invitation to join Friends on Holiday

"Trewartha",
Penkenna Haven,
Cornwall.
(*Date in full*).

Dear Marjorie,

As I told you, when we last met, we have taken a cottage in Cornwall for the whole of the school holidays. We have been here a fortnight now and are enjoying ourselves immensely. The children want nothing but the beach, of course, and I must say it is delightful to laze there in the sun, with a little surf-bathing to give one an appetite for a picnic lunch. So far, the weather has been brilliant, and the scenery is quite magnificent; since much of it is National Trust property, it cannot be spoiled by building.

Now my main reason for writing is this: we all hope very much that you and Peter can come and stay with us for a week, or better still, a fortnight. We shall be here until September 16th so do try and fit it in some time before then. I think we can really promise you a good time.

Yours ever,
Beryl Morrison.

No. 25.—Reply to above

300 High Street,
Guildford, Surrey.
(*Date in full*).

Dear Beryl,

I was delighted to have your letter and to know that your holiday is proving so successful. How very kind of you to think of Peter and myself; we shall be delighted to stay with you. Peter is busy at the office until August 23rd, but then has a fortnight free, so we will motor down on that Saturday and hope to arrive about tea-time. We are both looking forward to it tremendously.

Yours affectionately,
MARJORIE JAMES.

No. 26.—Invitation to join a motor tour

HOLLOWBURY,
WARWICK.

(*Date in full*).

DEAR JOAN,

My sister and I have decided to spend our holidays together next month motoring on the continent (using her car). As we shall have a spare seat, we wondered whether you would care to join us? Our provisional plan is to start on the 15th and to go via Paris, where we hope to look up some friends, and then down to the South of France and by easy stages across Italy, spending about three weeks in all. We hope to get hotel accommodation without advance booking, as it is early in the season, but thought of taking a tent and spirit stove so that we could camp out if we feel like it. We don't want to be tied to advance bookings but just go as the spirit moves us!

As we shall be making an early start on the 15th, could you come and stay the night here on the 14th? We do both hope that you are free and will feel tempted to join us.

On the question of expenses: as we shall be going anyway, we would not look for any contribution towards the costs of the car from you, but as regards hotel charges, meals out and similar expenses we plan to adopt the "Dutch treat" principle.

My love to your mother and father, and my sister asks to be kindly remembered to you all.

Yours ever,
ALISON.

No. 27.—Reply to above

ENDSLEIGH MANOR,
HERTFORD.
(*Date in full*).

DEAR ALISON,

What a very thrilling suggestion! I have always longed to revisit Paris where I spent a happy holiday as a schoolgirl, and Italy will be a new and wonderful experience. It is most kind of you to suggest my joining you. I have delayed replying for a day or so as I had to see my employer and make sure he did not mind my taking three weeks holiday all at once; the usual arrangement in the firm is one week in the spring and a fortnight later. However, he was quite sympathetic and agreed to waive the regulations for once, so now I can enthusiastically accept your very kind invitation. I am already taking steps to brush up my foreign languages in readiness! Please tell your sister how much I look forward to seeing her again, as we haven't met since that day at Cambridge.

My mother and father send their love.

Yours with excited anticipation,
JOAN.

No. 28.—Reply, refusing

ENDSLEIGH MANOR,
HERTFORD.
(*Date in full*).

MY DEAR ALISON,

How very kind of you to suggest including me in your holiday plans. I'm very very sorry, however, that I shall have to refuse your invitation.

The fact is that I have already made bookings to take Mother to Scotland just at that very time. I feel she really needs the holiday, and father won't hear of being away from his beloved garden in the summer. Mother won't go away alone so it has rather devolved upon me to see that she gets a rest and break from running the home. I need hardly tell you how disappointed I am that things have worked out like this; Scotland is all very well in its way, but not to be compared with Italy. However, that's life! By the by, I have not mentioned this to mother or father; I would not like them to think they have unwittingly caused me any disappointment.

Your affectionate,
JOAN.

No. 29.—Invitation to stay in Town

750 WILTON PLACE,
S.W.1.

(*Date in full*).

MY DEAR ALICE,

It seems a very long time since you were here and I am just longing to see you again. Letters are all very well but no substitute for a real "heart to heart" talk with all the odd bits of family news and a good laugh over old times.

Can you come and stay for a week or longer during the next school holidays? I'm sure after dealing with your class you will be ready for a rest, and I can promise you breakfast in bed and a few frivolous outings to the shops, with perhaps a theatre or two if you feel like it (there are a few good plays on just now).

Let me know if you can come, and when I can expect you. If it is to be during the week of April 13th-20th, be sure to bring a dance dress as George's Masonic Ladies Night falls in that week.

Now do try to come. We look forward to seeing you.

Yours affectionately,
MARY HALLIBURTON.

No. 30.—Reply

79 TITHE STREET,
IPSWICH.
(*Date in full*).

MY DEAR MARY,

Thank you for your letter and its kind invitation. I really *ought* to stay at home, as I have promised some of my girls a little extra coaching for their exam in June. However, your invitation sounds so tempting that I have persuaded myself that both they and I will work all the better afterwards for a week's break, and that a taste of the diversions of town is just what a teacher needs to keep things in proportion. In short, I accept with much pleasure.

I really think April 13th-20th would suit me best, as it is clear of the Easter travelling rush. I've chosen some heavenly brocade for a new dance dress and my "little woman" is making it up for me.

All news when we meet. Till then, the thought of seeing you is just what I need to cheer me for the rest of this tedious term.

Yours affectionately,
ALICE CHILWORTH.

No. 31.—From a Lady reminding another of a Former Friendship and seeking to renew it

GRASMERE,
HIGH WYCOMBE.
(*Date in full*).

DEAR MISS SEDGELEY,

I wonder if you will remember me? It seems a long time since we were at school together at Redbourne House, yet in other ways memories of those days are so fresh and vivid, for me at any rate, that it is hard to believe that so much has happened since then.

When my husband told me that he had met your brother at his club and learned from him that you are thinking of settling in this neighbourhood, I was delighted at the thought that this might perhaps mean the chance of seeing more of one another from now on, for I always regretted that our lives took such different paths once schooldays were ended.

If you are house-hunting in this district, it would give my husband and myself great pleasure if you would stay with us for a few days, which would perhaps give you time for a more leisurely inspection of the possibilities than one can get by merely visiting a district on brief excursions. Even if that is not possible, I do hope you will call on us one day for luncheon or tea when you are in the neighbourhood.

We are very quiet and have plenty of room and you could be free to come and go without ceremony according to the demands of your house-hunting timetable.

Yours sincerely,
ALICE POOLE (nee Stringer).

No. 32.—Answer affirmatively

HILLSIDE,
STREATHAM, S.W.
(*Date in full*).

DEAR ALICE (I can't bring myself to call you Mrs. Poole!),

Indeed I have not forgotten our schooldays, nor the many kindnesses you showed me then. Such memories become almost more cherished as time passes.

I thought of writing to you when my brother told me of his meeting with your husband, but frankly, did not want to obtrude the claims of an old friendship when you might by now have other demands on your time and good nature. So you can imagine how delighted I was to have your letter, and felt I simply must sit down and answer it right away.

My brother and I haven't absolutely decided on your neighbourhood, but we do like what we hear of it and your kind invitation will give us the chance to see more of it. I shall therefore take you at your word and come on Thursday next, arriving about 2 p.m.; unless some other day or time would be more convenient to you. My brother thanks you for your invitation to him; he will be kept in town by business until Saturday but would like to take advantage of your invitation to stay and proposes arriving on Saturday about 3—again, if that is not inconvenient.

Yours sincerely,
HELEN SEDGELEY.

No. 33—Reply, negatively

HILLSIDE,
STREATHAM, S.W.
(*Date in full*).

DEAR MRS. POOLE,

How very pleasant it was to receive your letter and to know that you still remember our former friendship, as I do.

It is most kind of you to invite my brother and myself to stay with you, but I am afraid I must regretfully decline. Our plans are still so vague that I would not feel justified in putting you to any inconvenience in the matter, though, believe me, I do appreciate the kind thought which prompted your suggestion.

With very many thanks for your kindness in asking me.

Yours sincerely,
HELEN SEDGELEY.

No. 34.—Postponing a visit

54 High Tree Rise,
Beckenham, Kent.
(*Date in full*).

My dear Frances,

I hardly know how to put this and I am so sorry to have to write at all, but I am afraid I must ask you to postpone your visit to us next week. Mother has succumbed to the current wave of influenza and I'm sorry to say that it has turned to pneumonia. Our doctor has been most helpful and I think she will pull through, but she will need careful nursing for quite a while and you will understand that my first thought must be for her just now.

Forgive my not writing more just now.

Yours as always,
Susan.

No. 35.—Offer to help a Friend in an Emergency

7 Holly Row,
Hampstead, N.W.3.
(*Date in full*).

My dear Susan,

We were all so very sorry to learn of your dear mother's illness. Do please give her our love and assure her that we are thinking of her and praying for a speedy recovery. Do not worry about any change of plan concerning myself for I quite realise that an illness of this nature must drive other concerns into the background.

Can I, though, be of any help to you if I come? I realise your mother will want you to nurse her, but I could at least relieve you of shopping, preparing the meals and answering the telephone. I am a reasonably good cook and can wield a duster with the best; do let me know if I may come and help. Don't bother with a long letter when you are so busy; just a postcard saying "Come" will do.

With love,
FRANCES.

No. 36.—Asking a Friend to call upon another Friend of the Writer

1 UTTERTON GARDENS,
LIVERPOOL 17.
(*Date in full*).

MY DEAR MARGARET,

Some friends and neighbours of ours, Mr. and Mrs. Livingstone, have recently moved near you, and it would please them and ourselves so much if you could manage to call upon them. They showed us much kindness when we first came to this district. Mr. Livingstone is in the legal profession. His wife is a very warm-hearted woman, and very musical. I would not ask you to do this if I did not feel that you will like them as much as we do and consider them a real acquisition to your neighbourhood.

I hope you are all well. We have had the usual colds that are so common at this time of year, but otherwise are very fit. Henry joins in sending kindest regards to you both.

Yours sincerely,
IRENE DOVE.

No. 37.—Reply to above

17 LAUREL MANSIONS,
CHESTER.
(*Date in full*).

MY DEAR IRENE,

I have delayed replying to your letter until I have had the chance to call upon the Livingstones as you asked me to do. I went yesterday and found Mrs. Livingstone at home. Joan, who came with me, and I, both thought her very delightful and the daughter, too, is charming; they have promised to bring Mr. Livingstone over for coffee with us one evening next week and I feel sure we shall be excellent friends. Perhaps one day, before too long, you will come over and meet them for luncheon at our house.

Arthur asks me to send his very kind regards, and Joan and I send love to you and Muriel.

Yours,
MARGARET BURNS.

No. 38.—Another reply

17 LAUREL MANSIONS,
CHESTER.

(*Date in full*).

MY DEAR IRENE,

In compliance with your request to call upon the Livingstones, I went yesterday, with Joan. I'm afraid we were not quite so enthusiastic about them as we had expected to be, although I'm sure they are very kind good people; perhaps they are still feeling unsettled from the effects of the move, or for some reason were not at their best. I have asked them to come one evening for coffee; this I felt I owed to you and your friendship for them. Perhaps we shall then get to know them better and the acquaintance may improve. But I don't honestly think we shall be very intimate friends. Perhaps, however, we may be helpful in tiding them over the first period of strangeness in a new district. For your sake, I very much hope so.

Yours always,
MARGARET BURNS.

ANNOUNCEMENTS AND LETTERS OF CONGRATULATION AND CONDOLENCE

No. 39.—Announcing an Engagement

The engagement is announced between Ernest George, only son of Mr. and Mrs. Arthur Smith of The Hollies, Rickmansworth, and Eileen Gwendoline, younger daughter of Mr. and Mrs. Reginald Westcott of 22 Chester Road, Brighton.

(Note: this form of announcement is used for publication in a newspaper.)

No. 40.—Announcing a Birth

ELM LODGE,
HARROGATE.

(*Date in full*).

DEAR MRS. WEST,

I know you will be pleased to hear that my sister has a beautiful boy. He was born at 8.30 this morning, and you can imagine the rejoicings. Both mother and child are doing well, I'm glad to say.

With love,
Yours affectionately,

MABEL LYTTON.

No. 41.—Congratulations on the Birth of a Child

CAMELOT,
DEVONSHIRE ROAD,
WIMBLEDON, S.W.19.

DEAR EMMA AND JOHN,

Please accept my very sincere congratulations upon the

safe arrival of your little son. You must both be very very happy indeed, and believe me, this is only the beginning, for from now on every day will bring fresh interest, entertainment, fresh developments and the kind of laughter that only parents can know. I am so very glad for you both.

Yours sincerely,
DOROTHY ELLERMAN.

No. 42.—Congratulations upon an Engagement

7 CLARENCE ROAD,
EXETER.

(*Date in full*).

MY DEAR BETTY,

I have just heard of your engagement and felt I must send you both my very best wishes for your future happiness and say how extremely delighted I am at this news. I am sure you will find much happiness together.

I shall look forward to hearing from you soon, and in the meantime, love and all good wishes.

from
JANE.

No. 43.—Reply to above

50 KING STREET,
S.W.3.

(*Date in full*).

MY DEAR JANE,

Thank you for your sweet note. Yes, Jack and I are very happy—we feel we can hardly believe it ourselves! But it does seem to be actually true, for we are already in the throes of house-hunting and if we can find a place that we like, shall plan our wedding to take place quite shortly.

I hope we shall meet soon for I have so much to tell you.

With love
BETTY.

No. 44.—Congratulations on a Professional Success

DOWNSIDE,
HAWKHURST,
SUSSEX.

(*Date in full*).

MY DEAR ELIZABETH,

It was with some surprise and great pleasure that I read in the paper the announcement of your appointment as Matron of the South Sussex Hospital. My dear, this is an achievement indeed, for one so young as yourself. I know all your friends will rejoice at your success, understanding, as we all do, how hard you have worked and how much you deserve this recognition. My earnest hope is that this appointment will give you ever greater scope for helping others, in the work to which you are devoting yourself.

Yours very sincerely,
JANE HOWARD.

No. 45.—Congratulations upon an Honour

THE OLD VICARAGE,
WHITCHURCH, MIDDLESEX.

(*Date in full*).

MY DEAR MISS STUBBINGS,

Please accept my very sincere congratulations upon receiving the award of the M.B.E. in the Birthday Honours List. Knowing you, I know that the voluntary work you have undertaken, of teaching music to inmates of prisons, is far more important to you than any recognition you may gain through it. Still, it is splendid to know that your work has not gone unrecognised, and that for once, merit has been rewarded. All your friends, I know, are so very delighted at this well-deserved honour.

Yours very sincerely,
VALERIE SIMPSON.

No. 46.—Letter of Condolence

200 PORTMAN GARDENS,
LONDON, W.1.
(*Date in full*).

MY DEAR JANE,

It was a great grief and shock to learn of the passing of your dear mother. Although it is a blessing that she is spared further suffering after so long an illness, still, for you and your family there is bound to be an overwhelming sorrow at losing her.

My husband and I will always cherish the memory of her as a charming and kindly hostess when we visited her—she had a wonderful gift for making everyone around her happy, and such a delightful sense of humour.

Please accept our very sincere condolences and loving thoughts to you all at this sad time.

Yours very sincerely,
MARY RENFREW.

No. 47.—Reply to same

MAYFIELD COTTAGE,
ROSE LANE,
TWICKENHAM.
(*Date in full*).

MY DEAR MARY,

Thank you for your kind letter. Mother's death has been an overwhelming blow to us all, but we are finding consolation in knowing that her suffering is over, and in knowing, too, that so many friends are holding us in their thoughts and prayers.

Yours sincerely,
JANE MARTIN.

No. 48.—Condolence. (More distant)

73 IRETON ROAD,
HOVE, SUSSEX.
(*Date in full*).

DEAR MRS. BROWN,

My husband and I were so very sad to hear of your bereavement, and hope you will accept our most sincere condolences.

Mr. Brown will be sadly missed by all who were privileged to know him, for he did so much good, both in his capacity as a Councillor, and as a private citizen and friend to so many.

Please accept this expression of our very deep sympathy with you and your family.

Yours very sincerely,
GLADYS SCRUTTON.

No. 49—Reply to above

4 REGENT TERRACE,
BRIGHTON.
(*Date in full*).

DEAR MRS. SCRUTTON,

Thank you so much for your kind expression of sympathy. It is a source of strength to know that so many kind friends are thinking of us just now.

Yours sincerely,
ELEANOR BROWN.

No. 50.—Condolence on the Death of a Child

THE DELL,
NORWOOD, S.W.23.
(*Date in full*).

MY DEAR MADELEINE,

We are deeply and sincerely sorry for your great loss. Words just seem vain and useless in the face of what you are going through. It seems so terribly tragic to think of that bright little life cut short, and one is left wondering helplessly—Why? I can only pray that God will give you strength to bear this terrible blow. My husband joins with me in this; our thoughts and prayers are with you at this sad time.

I remain, my dear,
Your loving friend,
DILYS GREY.

No. 51.—Reply to above

7 DUKE OF YORK MANSIONS,
BATTERSEA, S.W.11.
(*Date in full*).

MY DEAR DILYS,

At this awful time of trial, it is a great help to know that friends are thinking of us and bearing us in their prayers. I cannot write more just now. I still feel completely stunned and bewildered. But thank you for your kind letter.

Yours with love,
MADELEINE RICHARDSON.

REQUESTS

No. 52.—From a Lady Asking Another to Help a Charity

THE GROVE,
LITTLE RUSTINGTON,
DORSET.

(*Date in full*).

DEAR MRS. THOMAS,

I wonder if I may trespass upon your kindness for the sake of a very worthy cause? The Little Rustington branch of the Refugee Children's Aid Society is holding a small garden fete on May 17th next; weather permitting it will be in the vicarage garden, which the Vicar is kindly lending, or alternatively in the church hall.

No doubt you already know of the good work of the R.C.A.S. but in case you do not, I enclose a leaflet describing the Society's activities which I feel sure you will agree deserve all our support.

The Committee would be so very pleased if you could be one of the stall-holders, or help in any other way. Will you let me know if you can do this? There is a preliminary meeting to discuss arrangements at the home of our chairman, Miss Smith, next Tuesday, and I do hope you will be able to be present.

Yours sincerely,
JANE FEVEREL.

No. 53.—Reply to above

HIGHFIELD COTTAGE,
GREAT RUSTINGTON,
DORSET.

(*Date in full*).

DEAR MRS. FEVEREL,

Thank you for your letter about the fete in aid of the Refugee Children's Aid Society. I shall be very happy to do what I can to help this excellent cause, and will look forward to attending the preliminary meeting at Miss Smith's next Tuesday.

Yours sincerely,
ELIZABETH THOMAS.

No. 54.—Another Reply

HIGHFIELD COTTAGE,
GREAT RUSTINGTON,
DORSET.

(*Date in full*).

DEAR MRS. FEVEREL,

Thank you for your letter about the fete in aid of the Refugee Children's Aid Society. I should have liked to help, but frankly, have so many calls upon my time just at present that I am unable to undertake anything more at the moment. I enclose a small contribution to the funds, with my best wishes for the success of the function. If you are able to let me have more copies of the leaflet, I will do my best to make the affair known among those who may be able to support it.

Yours sincerely,
ELIZABETH THOMAS.

No. 55.—Request to a Lady to Serve on a Committee

THE GROVE,
LITTLE RUSTINGTON,
DORSET.

(*Date in full*).

DEAR MRS. THOMAS,

I know how many calls you have upon your time, but I am wondering if you would feel able to undertake one more activity in a very worthy cause.

As you perhaps know, Jane Smith is leaving the district, and this leaves a vacancy upon the committee of our local branch of the Refugee Children's Aid Society, which Jane helped to start.

It has been suggested that you might be willing to serve upon this committee—we do need somebody active and with lots of good ideas, to take her place! Should you feel able to undertake this, it would entail a monthly committee meeting and some work in connection with our annual fête.

If you are willing to be co-opted to the committee I will bring forward your name at the next meeting.

Yours sincerely,
JANE FEVEREL.

No. 56.—Reply

HIGHFIELD COTTAGE,
GREAT RUSTINGTON,
DORSET.

(*Date in full*).

DEAR MRS. FEVEREL,

Thank you for your letter about the R.C.A.S. Jane Smith will be greatly missed and it will be no easy task for anyone to take her place, but if you think I can help I shall be most happy to serve in any way I can. No doubt you will be letting me know if the matter is confirmed by the committee.

Yours sincerely,
ELIZABETH THOMAS.

No. 57.—Request to a Lady to Open a Fête

THE GROVE,
LITTLE RUSTINGTON,
DORSET.

(*Date in full*).

DEAR LADY CUMMINGS,

The Little Rustington branch of the Refugee Children's Aid Society is planning to hold a small garden fête in May and the Committee would feel honoured if you would agree to perform the opening ceremony.

No doubt you already know of this worthy cause which for some years now has brought help and comfort in varied ways, to those who are suffering through no fault of their own. I enclose one of the most recent leaflets about the work. We want to make our fête a really successful effort and the presence of yourself as patron would undoubtedly be a very great help to the cause.

We have not finally settled upon the actual date, as knowing how busy your ladyship is, we felt it might be preferable for you to name the most convenient day. The Vicar has kindly agreed to lend us the Vicarage garden on any day in the second half of May.

May we hope that you will help our cause in this way?

Yours truly,
JANE FEVEREL,
Hon. Sec.

No. 58.—Thanking a Lady for her Patronage of a Charity

THE GROVE,
LITTLE RUSTINGTON,
DORSET.
(*Date in full*).

DEAR LADY CUMMINGS,

The Committee have asked me to express to you their very sincere thanks for your gracious help in opening the fete for the Refugee Children last Saturday. Your help in this way not only contributed greatly towards the very successful financial result (the final sum collected is £147 10s.) but much enhanced the pleasure of the occasion for everyone. Thank you so much.

Yours sincerely,
JANE FEVEREL,
Hon. Sec.

No. 59.—From a Lady asking for Help at a Charity Bazaar

THE LARCHES,
HAWKMINSTER.
(*Date in full*).

DEAR MRS. LAMBERT,

I have undertaken to provide a "fish-pond" at the forthcoming annual bazaar in aid of our Cottage Hospital Amenities Fund, and I shall be very grateful if I may receive a contribution from you. We intend having "dips" from one penny to sixpence, and anything will be acceptable—fancy articles, ornaments, toys, packets of sweets, or money to provide materials.

Thanking you in anticipation

I am
Yours sincerely,
MARY WILLIS.

No. 60.—Asking for Votes for a Candidate for Admission to a Home

4 Springfield Terrace,
N.W.8.
(*Date in full*).

Dear Mr. Halford,

May I solicit your vote and interest on behalf of Miss Elsa Sprigge, whose admission into the South Eastern Home for Incurables I am anxious to secure? It is in every way a most deserving case, and if you have not already promised your support to another candidate I shall be most grateful if I may count upon your assistance for this unfortunate friend of mine. I will send you full particulars of her story if you wish to consider the relative claims of her and any other case, but for the present, as the election is still some time distant, I content myself with this brief appeal. I know that the weight of your name would help materially to turn the scale in her favour.

I am
Yours sincerely,
Julia Martin.

No. 61.—Letter of Introduction

Ash Villa,
Sidney Road,
Clacton-on-Sea.
(*Date in full*).

My dear Joan,

Bringing this letter is Miss Pamela English, the daughter of a close friend of mine who, like so many young people nowadays, is spending a year seeing something of the world, including Australia.

Pamela is a delightful girl. I feel sure you will all like her as much as we do. Anything you can do to help her meet congenial young people of her own age, and to make friends, will be tremendously appreciated by her and, I need hardly add, by me. I feel sure it will be reassuring to her, as well as enjoyable, to meet someone like yourself with whom she can talk about England.

John sends his kind regards; I will write you a really long newsy letter in a week or two; just now I am in a tremendous rush getting the children ready to go back to school.

With love,
FIONA.

No. 62.—Reply to above

LEGANA,
YEW TREE ROAD,
MELBOURNE.
(*Date in full*).

MY DEAR FIONA,

It was a real pleasure to get your letter brought by Pamela—you see I don't call her Miss English, for we got on the most friendly terms right away. We all found her charming and enjoyed seeing her photos of you and the children and hearing her news of you all. As you know, I always love to meet someone from the Old Country. Pamela is coming out here again next weekend when we hope to have a small party of young neighbours of about her own age so that she can meet some congenial people.

We have no special news. It has been a hard winter here but Spring seems to be coming at last—and Ted is keenly looking forward to the arrival of the English Test Team for the forthcoming series!

Yours with love,
JOAN.

No. 63.—Thanks for Letter of Introduction

KOOKABURRA HOTEL,
MELBOURNE.

(*Date in full*).

DEAR MRS. MULHOLLAND,

I want to thank you again for the introduction you so kindly gave me to Joan and Ted Richardson. I made a point of getting in touch with them almost as soon as I arrived in Melbourne, and they at once invited me to spend the following Sunday with them. We had a most enjoyable talk and they made me most welcome, in that lovely homely Australian way. They have arranged a little party for me and you can imagine how much I am looking forward to this. Australia is an interesting country, so very different from England that I find it a bit bewildering still. However, now that I have some real friends here I am beginning to feel much more at home.

Yours very sincerely,
PAMELA ENGLISH.

No. 64.—Letter of Thanks for Kindness shown to a Friend

ASH VILLA,
SIDNEY ROAD,
CLACTON-ON-SEA.

(*Date in full*).

MY DEAR JOAN,

I want to thank you very sincerely for your kind reception of Pamela English. Of course it is only what I expected from two such warm-hearted people as yourself and Ted, but it is none the less appreciated. I know that the reception you gave Pamela must have been a tremendous help to her in settling down. Thank you both so much.

With love,
FIONA.

ENGAGEMENT AND MARRIAGE

No. 65.—Accepting a Proposal by Letter

FIRTREE COTTAGE,
MARLOW.

(*Date in full*).

MY DEAREST ROBERT,

Your dear letter was indeed a surprise, a very very wonderful one I admit, but my mind is in such a turmoil that I hardly know how to sort out my thoughts and feelings. Perhaps I had better come to the point straight away and tell you that the answer is "yes". And thank you, my dear, for paying me this wonderful compliment of asking me to be your wife.

Of course I knew before you went abroad that I was growing more and more fond of you, and you made it plain that you felt the same about me. But marriage is such a big step, and I did not know whether your new life and interests abroad, and the fact of not seeing one another for some time, might make you think differently about everything. Now that we both know that our feelings have stood the test of separation, I think we can be sure that we really *are* meant for one another for all our future lives.

I have, of course, told my parents of your letter; although owing to your being away it isn't possible for you to have the traditional formal little interview with Daddy at the moment, I know he would welcome a letter from you.

Forgive a longer letter now, dearest. My mind is in such a whirl of happy thoughts I can't write coherently. How I long to see you again! I must console myself with the thought that every day brings your return a little nearer.

With all my love,
Always your own,
MARJORIE.

No. 66.—Another ditto

ADA VILLA,
CARIS ROAD,
SOUTHAMPTON.
(*Date in full*).

MY DEAREST JACK,

It would be hard to describe my feelings since your letter came. I think I must be the happiest girl alive and so proud that you have asked me to be your wife. My dear, yes, with all my heart. I can tell you now that I have loved you ever since we first met, and my whole life shall be passed in trying to show you how real and true my love is.

If only you had not to be away just now. Still, as it has meant this wonderful new job of yours which is going to make it possible for us to marry, I suppose I must not grumble at this little separation. I expect when you come back you will want to see father (I know he will want to see you—but don't worry, he isn't so alarming as you probably think!) and tell him of your plans. He will be so pleased to hear of this success of yours, and I know he will help us both as far as he can.

I just can't find words for all that is in my heart. So come back soon, the very instant your conferences and meetings are over. There is so much to talk about and to plan for.

Your own,
SANDRA.

No. 67.—Refusing a Proposal of Marriage

THE TOWERS,
LANCASTER ROAD,
GOLDERS GREEN.
(*Date in full*).

DEAR JOHN,

I was rather surprised to get your letter. Although I had, of course, realised that you singled me out from other girls, I did not think I had given you any encouragement to do so, or that you were so serious in your feelings about me as I now realise from your letter you are.

What I have to say is, I fear, bound to be hurtful to you, John, and I wish for your sake that I did not have to do this. I do not reciprocate your feelings and I don't think I could ever consent to be your wife. We are too different in character, background, temperament, everything; we could never find lasting happiness together. I know this will be a blow to you just now, but I sincerely hope that you will come to see that I am right and that, as time goes on, you will find someone more suited than I am to make you a loving wife and helpmeet.

You will understand when I say that it will be wisest if we avoid meeting, as far as possible, for the time being. It could only be hurtful.

Yours very sincerely,
EMMA ANDERSON.

No. 68.—Letter from a Daughter Announcing her Engagement

67 Tower Mansions,
Finchley, N.3.
(*Date in full*).

Dearest Daddy,

I have a very important piece of news to tell you and I do hope that you will be pleased and happy about it. As you know, Harry Dare and I have been friends for some time, and now he has asked me to marry him. He is a very nice boy and I do indeed feel I love him and want to be his wife.

Harry is in a steady job with excellent prospects with a very good firm; but he will explain all that to you when I bring him to meet you. You and Mummy have always said you wanted my happiness and I think I can honestly say that my happiness will be with Harry. I know you are going to like him as much as I do.

I will bring Harry home with me when I come in a fortnight's time, and I do hope that you will give your approval to our announcing our engagement.

Your loving daughter,
Kathleen.

No. 69.—Another ditto

Holmwood,
17 Brighton Square,
London, N.W.2.
(*Date in full*).

My dearest Mother and Daddy,

When I left home to come to England, I suppose we all

knew that big changes might take place before we met again, and now I have some important and exciting news which I hope will make you as happy as it makes me.

I've written previously about Michael Anderson, and you have probably guessed that we were becoming rather special friends. Now Michael has asked me to marry him and I have said yes. He is a dear boy—I only wish I could introduce him to you, for I know you would like him every bit as much as I do.

Knowing how you both worry about my welfare here, I am afraid this news is going to cause you a little anxiety. Believe me, it need not. Michael is in a good job and intends to work hard and get on; and we have been friends long enough to know our own minds very well. We both know things may not always be easy but we are confident that together we can overcome all difficulties.

Our plan is to be married early in the New Year. If, though, there is any chance of you coming over here for the wedding, we would fix the date so as to link up with whatever time you could arrange to come. To have you with us on the great day, sharing our happiness, is just the one thing needed to make it complete.

I will write again soon and send a photo of Michael. Do let me know that you are pleased at my news.

Your loving daughter,
DOROTHY.

No. 70.—From a Young Lady to her Sweetheart

69 THE CRESCENT,
IPSWICH.

(*Date in full*).

MY DEAR ROBERT,

Although I have written to you each week, it is now a

month since I heard from you, and it worries me very much to think something may be wrong. I do hope that all is well with you, that you are not ill or anxious about anything; do write and let me know, for perhaps I can help, or at any rate, sharing your troubles is bound to lighten them. Otherwise, I can only conclude either that you do not know how much I miss hearing from you and how unkind of you I feel it, not to have written; or else that you don't care. Now do please write soon, for I am really worried.

Yours always,
HELEN FOSTER.

No. 71.—Another

"SEA VIEW",
MOLESWORTH CRESCENT,
BOGNOR REGIS.
(*Date in full*).

MY DEAR PHILIP,

I can hardly believe you wrote the letter which I received this morning. It is so different from your usual cheery scrawl that it makes me feel it comes from a stranger, not from you at all. If there is some reason for the change in you, I beg you to let me know, for perhaps we could clear up the misunderstanding. If, as I must conclude unless you give me some explanation, your feelings towards me have changed, then please do not bother to write again; I could not wish to hold you against your will. I am very hurt by the tone of your letter, but perhaps it is as well that we have both found out our true feelings now, rather than later.

Yours very sincerely,
CICELY HAMILTON.

No. 72.—Breaking an Engagement

5 The Crescent,
Bannow.

(*Date in full*).

My dear James,

I can understand your letter, although I admit I had expected and hoped for something different. Your feelings to me have changed—I have sensed as much for some time—and only the fact that our engagement has been announced, stops you from making a break. I appreciate your honourable attitude over this, but believe me, I could not wish to proceed with our plans, knowing that you have changed as you have. Please feel released from our engagement, and accept the return of your ring and letters which I now enclose.

Although I feel horribly upset over this turn of events, in a way it is a relief to have things clear after the uncertainty of the last few weeks. I shall always wish you well, but I feel it will be for the best if we do not meet again.

Yours sincerely,
Margaret Denton.

No. 73.—Condolence upon a Broken Engagement

200 Charles Street,
W.1.

(*Date in full*).

My dear May,

I have just heard of the sad experience you have been through in the breaking off of your engagement. I was so very sorry as I know how happy you used to be with Philip and what plans you were making. However, I must admit that for some little time I had felt you were not as happy as formerly. I trust that time will heal your wound and that, as is so often the case, things will prove to have turned out for the best. Believe me, all your friends think of you with love and sympathy.

Yours always,
MOLLY.

No. 74.—Renewing an Engagement

5 THE CRESCENT,
BANNOW.

(*Date in full*).

MY DEAR JAMES,

Your letter made me so happy and I realise how terribly mistaken I was in thinking you wished to break our engagement. If only you had told me of your difficulties, the whole misunderstanding might have been saved, and I would have been so proud to share your troubles and perhaps help you out of them. Come and see me as soon as you can; there is so much to talk over and I'm longing to greet you again in the old way and for things to be just as they always were.

Always your own,
MARGARET.

No. 75.—Letter to a Prospective Son-in-Law

17 NORTH ROAD,
CHEPSTOW.

(*Date in full*).

MY DEAR HOWARD,

Jennifer has written telling us of your engagement and although we shall be seeing you both at the weekend I felt I must write at once to tell you how happy my husband and I are at this news. There is nobody we would rather have for a son-in-law than yourself and we welcome the closer link that this will mean with your own family. After being friends for so long, we are now to be actually related!

I am writing to your mother, and hope that she and Mr. Evans will be able to motor over on Saturday as I'm sure we shall all have a lot to talk about then.

Yours affectionately,
MARY HANKINSON.

No. 76.—Letter to Prospective In-laws

17 NORTH ROAD,
CHEPSTOW.

(*Date in full*).

MY DEAR MRS. EVANS,

I daresay by now you have heard from Howard of his engagement to Jennifer—not that it was exactly a surprise to us, and no doubt you, too, were well aware of what was in the wind!

John and I are so happy about it; we have always thought Howard a fine boy and just the kind of son we would have liked to have ourselves.

The two young people are coming down here to stay at the weekend, and it would give us all so much pleasure if you and Mr. Evans could motor over here for luncheon on Saturday. I daresay we shall all have plenty to talk about.

With kindest regards to yourself and Mr. Evans.

Yours sincerely,
MARY HANKINSON.

No. 77.—Letter to a Prospective Daughter-in-Law

19 ROSS ROAD,
HEREFORD.

(*Date in full*).

MY DEAR JENNIFER,

Howard has told me of your engagement, and although I hope to see you very soon, I must write at once to tell you how pleased Howard's father and I are, and how happy it has made us.

We very much hope that Howard will bring you to see us quite soon as we are greatly looking forward to hearing more about your future plans and welcoming you to our family as a prospective daughter-in-law.

Till then, my dear, we both send every good wish for your future happiness.

Yours sincerely,
SUSAN EVANS.

No. 78.—Ditto (more distant)

19 ROSS ROAD,
HEREFORD.

(*Date in full*).

MY DEAR JENNIFER,

Howard has told me of your engagement and although I hope very soon to make your acquaintance in person I felt I must write at once to welcome you as a future member of our family. I hope that Howard will bring you down here to see us as soon as possible. In the meantime, please accept our good wishes for your happiness as our boy's wife.

Yours sincerely,
SUSAN EVANS.

No. 79.—Letter to Prospective In-laws

19 Ross Road,
Hereford.

(*Date in full*).

Dear Mrs. Hankinson,

It made me very happy when Howard told me that Jennifer had agreed to marry him and that you and Mr. Hankinson had given the engagement your blessing, for I have realised for some time how much Jennifer meant to him.

My husband and I lead such a quiet life and go out so little that we haven't had the opportunity of making your acquaintance hitherto, but now that we are actually to be related, this must be remedied as soon as possible! Would you and Mr. Hankinson do us the honour of dining with us next Thursday? It would give us so much pleasure. Seven o'clock for seven-thirty, and dress informal as there will be just the four of us.

Yours sincerely,
Susan Evans.

No. 80.—Reply to above

17 North Road,
Chepstow.

(*Date in full*).

Dear Mrs. Evans,

Thank you for your charming letter. My husband and I are very happy about the children's engagement—we have long had great admiration for Howard and now look forward to getting to know his family too. It is most kind of you to ask us to dine on Thursday and we accept with pleasure.

Yours very sincerely,
Mary Hankinson.

No. 81.—Letter to Accompany reply to a Wedding Invitation

19 KING'S ROAD,
CHEPSTOW.

(*Date in full*).

MY DEAR MARY,

In accepting (or, in refusing) yours and Harry's invitation to Jennifer's wedding, I feel I must send a little note to say how very happy I am that the dear child is to be married, and to such a fine young man. It seems no time since she was a schoolgirl in short gym tunic, and now to be a bride! It makes me feel quite old to think of how these children grow up. I know, as a parent myself, that you and Harry must be happy that she is to be comfortably settled. Believe me, all your friends share in your joy.

Affectionately,
ELLA JENKINS.

No. 82.—Letter Postponing a Wedding Invitation

17 NORTH ROAD,
CHEPSTOW.

(*Date in full*).

MY DEAR FLORENCE,

I am sorry to tell you that Jennifer's marriage to Howard on the 25th of this month is postponed. His mother has been taken quite seriously ill; in fact the doctor cannot say with certainty that she will be out of danger for some weeks to come. In the circumstances, we have felt it only right to postpone the ceremony. I will write again later and hope then to be able to tell you that all is well and that we have fixed a fresh date for the wedding.

Yours sincerely,
MARY HANKINSON.

No. 83.—Letter of Thanks for Wedding Present

17 North Road,
Chepstow.
(*Date in full*).

Dear Mrs. Ellis,

Thank you so much for your beautiful present and the very kind letter which came with it. The little table is absolutely charming and I am simply longing to see it in its proper setting, in our own home. Howard likes it as much as I do and asks me to thank you on his behalf.

Yours sincerely,
Jennifer Hankinson.

BUSINESS

No. 84.—Stopping Payment of a Cheque

The Yews,
Berkhamsted.
(*Date in full*).

The Manager,
West Herts Bank Ltd.,
Watford.

Sir,

Please stop payment of my cheque No. L000 for £62 10s. 0d. dated the 16th inst, drawn in favour of Arthur Brown and signed by myself.

Yours faithfully,
Phyllis Morton.

No. 85.—Enclosing Cheque for Account of Third Party

17 Somerset Road,
Leeds.

(*Date in full*).

The Manager,
The Yorkshire Bank Limited,
Leeds.

Dear Sir,

Enclosed please find cheque £100 which please place to the credit of your clients, Messrs. George Brown and Co.

Yours faithfully,
Irene Smith.

No. 86.—Opening another Account

24 Richmond Road,
Liverpool.

(*Date in full*).

Messrs. East Lancashire Bank Ltd.,
Exchange Chambers,
Dale Street,
Aintree,
Liverpool.

Dear Sirs,

I enclose cheque value £200 (two hundred pounds). Please place this to the credit of a new account to be opened under the name of "Edna B. Jones-Smith, 'B' Account". I trust you will be good enough to honour all cheques presented to you to the debit of the above account.

Yours faithfully,
Edna B. Jones-Smith.

No. 87.—Changing Doctors, Private

OAKLANDS,
GROVE ROAD,
CROYDON.

(*Date in full*).

DEAR DR. MILTON,

For some time I have not felt satisfied with the progress of Peter's illness, and rather than let things drag on in this way any longer, I think it might be wise to try a change of treatment. Thank you for all you have done for Peter. If you will kindly send your account, I will attend to it right away.

Yours truly,
JOAN HARRIS.

No. 88.—To a New Doctor, Private

OAKLANDS,
GROVE ROAD,
CROYDON.

(*Date in full*).

DEAR DR. PARRY,

Would you kindly call at this address as soon as possible? My son Peter, aged 11, has had a chest complaint for some time for which he has been attended by Dr. Milton. As things have not improved I feel it wise to try a change of treatment and have notified Dr. Milton accordingly. I should be glad if you would take charge of the case from now on.

Yours truly,
JOAN HARRIS.

No. 89.—Changing Doctors, National Health Service

20 CROSBY GARDENS,
NORTH FINCHLEY.
(*Date in full*).

DEAR DR. GROVE,

For some while I have not felt happy about my family's being on your list. Peter's cough, for example, has not improved as I feel it should. I realise you are a busy man and perhaps it would be better if we registered with another doctor who has rather more time for these obstinate cases. Will you therefore kindly accept this notification of our withdrawal from your list.

Yours faithfully,
MARY SAWTON.

No. 90.—To a New Doctor, National Health Service

20 CROSBY GARDENS,
NORTH FINCHLEY.
(*Date in full*).

DEAR DR. PARRY,

Would you kindly accept myself and my family (husband and three children) as patients on your list under the National Health Service? We were formerly patients of Dr. Milton, but have felt it wise for various reasons to make a change. I enclose our N.H.S. cards.

Yours faithfully,
MARY SAWTON.

No. 91.—Engaging a Solicitor

23 Everton Road,
Stanmore.
(*Date in full*).

Dear Sir,

Your name has been given to me by Mr. James Henderson, for whom I understand you act in legal matters. I need the help of a solicitor experienced in house purchase matters, and would be obliged if you would act for me in this and other concerns from now onwards. I look forward to hearing that you are able to do this.

Yours faithfully,
Joan Harris.

No. 92.—Changing a Solicitor

23 Everton Road,
Stanmore, Middx.
(*Date in full*).

Dear Sir,

As you know, I am the sole executor of the will drawn up by you for my aunt, Mrs. Sara Daw. As I live some distance from your city and find it difficult to make the necessary visits there I feel it would be best if this matter were handled by Messrs. Mann, Chandler, and Nephew, my own solicitors here. Will you kindly forward them the relevant papers? If you will let me have your account for the work already done in the matter, I will attend to it at once.

Yours faithfully,
Joan Harris.

No. 93.—Letter Respecting Lost Luggage

GROVE LODGE,
KENSINGTON, S.W.7.
(*Date in full*).

The Supervisor,
British Railways, North Western Region.

DEAR SIR,

I regret to have to inform you that a black leather trunk belonging to me was lost during the journey from Manchester to London by the train which arrived at Euston at 7 p.m. yesterday. I saw the trunk placed in the guard's van at Manchester, but when the train reached London it had disappeared. I notified the stationmaster's office of my loss at once. I should be glad if you would institute a thorough search for the missing property. The trunk, which was labelled with my name and the above address, contains silk dresses, underwear and shoes worth £25 and that is the amount which I shall claim from British Railways in the event of the search proving unsuccessful.

Yours faithfully,
MARY CLOGHAN.

No. 94.—Letter Asking for a Business Introduction

19 SELDON AVENUE,
LONDON, N.10.
(*Date in full*).

DEAR TOM,

I wonder if you would be kind enough to give me an introduction to Mr. Leslie Appleby whom I believe you know. I want to see him upon a business matter which I think may have certain advantages for him as well as for myself. I shall be so much obliged to you if you can bring about a meeting between us. And I need hardly say that if at any time I can help you in a similar way I shall be very pleased to do so.

Yours sincerely,
ALICE PATERSON.

No. 95.—To a Landlord about Repairs

3 MAYGROVE TERRACE,
LONDON, S.W.8.
(*Date in full*).

DEAR SIR,

I shall be glad if you will ask your representative to call and inspect my upper rooms with a view to some necessary repairs. Owing to a loose roofing tile, water found its way to the ceiling during the recent bad weather and caused several portions to fall, with some damage to the rooms below. I would also like your representative to see the dilapidated state of the kitchen, and the wallpaper of the sitting room. He promised to repair and improve the condition of the house when I became your tenant, but so far nothing has been done.

May this matter have your immediate attention?

Yours faithfully,
ELLEN KIRWAN.

No. 96.—Letter Requesting time to pay Rent

3 MAYGROVE TERRACE,
LONDON, S.W.8.
(*Date in full*).

DEAR SIR,

Owing to circumstances beyond my control (the strike of the Silk Thread Operatives Union, which had adverse repercussions on my dressmaking business) I find myself in temporary financial difficulties. I would regard it as a great favour if you will allow me to pay two quarters' rent together in March, that is, the sum now due and that due at Lady Day, making in all £50. Should things improve more rapidly, I will do what I can to send something on account before March, but in any event will meet the whole sum then.

Yours faithfully,
ELLEN KIRWAN.

No. 97.—Receipt for Rent

Received of Mrs. Margaret Doyle, the sum of £25 being one quarter's rent due on Lady Day last for the premises occupied by her at No. 300, Charles Street, W.1.

EVA JONES-SMITH
(*Date in full*).

No. 98.—To a Landlord asking for Release from an Agreement

28 THE VALE,
FULHAM, S.W.6.
(*Date in full*).

DEAR SIR,

The executors have now wound up the estate of my late husband and it is necessary for me to reduce my expenses drastically if I am to live within the income remaining to me. I must therefore, with great regret, seek a smaller house, and my object in writing is to ask if you will terminate the agreement you made with us. I realise I have power to sub-let the premises, but am reluctant to incur the responsibility which this would entail, and should therefore be so very grateful if you would allow me to vacate the house at Midsummer, instead of holding me to the strict letter of the contract.

Yours faithfully,
JANE FISHER.

No. 99.—To House Agent Stating Requirements

MILL LODGE,
GREEK STREET,
HERTFORD.
(*Date in full*).

DEAR SIRS,

I am anxious to rent a house, at not more than £400 a year, in the neighbourhood of Hendon. It should be in a quiet and cheerful road, with easy access to shops and public transport, and be suitable for entertaining. I need four bedrooms. I do not want a repairing lease.

Will you let me know of any houses you may have on your books which are likely to be suitable?

Yours faithfully,
MADELEINE SNOW.

No. 100.—To the Sanitary Inspector, Complaining of Defective Drains

GROVELANDS,
BINGHAM.
(*Date in full*).

DEAR SIR,

We have recently been troubled with an outbreak of sore throats in the family, and our medical man suggests that one possible cause might be some defect in the sanitary arrangements of this house. Will you, therefore, kindly send a competent person to test the drains thoroughly and communicate with the landlord in the event of any defect being discovered.

I am,
Yours faithfully,
KATE RISBEE.

No. 101.—Inquiring about Hotel Accommodation

7 FRENCH STREET,
N.W.5.

(*Date in full*).

To the Manager,
The Ship Hotel,
Brightlingsea.

DEAR SIR,

Your hotel has been recommended to me by a friend, Mrs. Jane Bowman. As I hope to come to Brightlingsea in June, would you kindly send me a note of your terms and also let me know whether you could let me have two double rooms facing the sea between June 12th and June 26th. One room would be for my husband and myself, the other for our two boys aged 5 and 7. Perhaps you would let me know if there is any reduction in terms for children. I would also like to know if there is any objection to our bringing our dog with us? He is quite well trained and would not upset other guests.

Yours faithfully,
MADGE SEAFORTH.

No. 102.—Reserving Hotel Accommodation

7 FRENCH STREET,
N.W.5.
(*Date in full*).

DEAR SIR,

Thank you for sending me your prospectus and a note of your terms. These are satisfactory, so will you please reserve for us the rooms mentioned in your letter. We shall motor down on June 12th, arriving about 4 p.m.

Yours truly,
MADGE SEAFORTH.

No. 103.—Booking a Steamer Passage

200 HANS PLACE,
LONDON, S.W.3.
(*Date in full*).

DEAR SIRS,

I wish to sail for New York in R.M.S. Majestia, arriving on or before June 10th. I shall require two 1st class passages. Would you kindly forward me particulars of stateroom accommodation and sailing dates?

Yours faithfully,
PHYLLIS BORDON.

The General Navigation Co. Ltd.,
300 Cockspur Street, S.W.1.

No. 104.—Booking Seats in Aeroplane

24 JAMES STREET,
BERKELEY SQUARE, W.1.
(*Date in full*).

DEAR SIR,

Confirming our telephone conversation of this morning, kindly reserve me two seats in the plane leaving London

Airport for Paris at 2 p.m. on Wednesday, June 12th. I shall also be glad if you will let me know the connections between London and the airport. I enclose cheque for the price of the seats.

Yours faithfully,
NATALIE BROCKLEHURST.

The Manager,
International Air Services Agency,
Regent Street, W.1.

No. 105.—Letter of Complaint

37 HOWARTH HILL,
S.E.6.

(*Date in full*).

DEAR SIR,

I regret exceedingly to have to make a complaint about some curtain material bought in your furnishing fabrics department six months ago.

The material, a silk and rayon mixture costing 10/11d. a yard, was made into curtains at once and two weeks ago they were taken down and sent to the cleaners. To my surprise, they returned almost in ribbons, and the cleaners disclaim liability, saying the damage is due to some fault in manufacture.

I feel there has been some bad mistake somewhere for this is not what one expects with goods bought at a reputable store such as yours. I shall be glad to know what you propose to do to put matters right.

Yours faithfully,
MARGARET GLENISTER.

The Manager,
Messrs. Harridge's Ltd.,
Oxford Street, W.1.

No. 106.—Another Complaint

RILSDALE,
DULWICH, S.E.21.
(*Date in full*).

DEAR SIR,

I much regret having to make a complaint but feel this matter should be brought to your attention.

Two nights ago, on December 15th, my husband and myself stayed at your hotel and were given Room No. 17. Our stay was completely ruined through the noise which went on in the room below for the greater part of the night. I understand Room 17 is over part of the service quarters and apparently some of the staff were on duty well into the small hours, and again from about 5.30. I quite realise that the organisation of the hotel may make this necessary, but I feel that if such work cannot be done in a room more remote from the guests' quarters, then at least firm measures should be taken to ensure that no unnecessary noise is made.

Perhaps you will let me have your comments.

Yours faithfully,
ETHEL BARRINGTON.

The Manager,
White Hart Hotel,
Edginford, Sussex.

No. 107.—Complaint to Local Authority

HURST MANOR,
INGLEWICK,
BARSETSHIRE.
(*Date in full*).

DEAR SIR,

I feel I must complain about the untidy and careless behaviour of the dustmen who collect our refuse. They take no trouble whatever to avoid spilling the contents of the dustbins, and the roadway after the dustcart has passed is in a most untidy and unpleasant condition. As a ratepayer I feel we are entitled to better service than this and ask you to take whatever steps are necessary to see that it does not happen in future.

Yours faithfully,
GLENDA MILLINGTON.

The Overseer,
Refuse Collection Dept.,
Inglewick U.D.C. Offices,
Barsetshire.

No. 108.—Letter to an Insurance Company

THE YEWS,
KING'S ROAD,
BOXMOOR.

(*Date in full*).

DEAR SIR,

I have just bought a Canadian Squirrel fur coat and wish to insure it against loss, theft, damage, etc. The cost of the coat and the sum for which I wish to insure it is £350. Will you kindly send your representative to arrange the terms of the insurance, and in the meantime I should be obliged if you would hold me covered as from the date of this letter.

Yours faithfully,
JENNIFER STRATTON.

The Manager,
Regal Insurance Company,
Lombard Street, E.C.

No. 109.—Letter Claiming from an Insurance Company

THE YEWS,
KINGS ROAD,
BOXMOOR.

(*Date in full*).

DEAR SIR,

I am sorry to tell you that on Thursday last, 15th May, a burglar entered my house while I was out at the theatre and stole the diamond ring, insured by you under Policy No.——. Nothing else was taken as the man was apparently disturbed before he could ransack the house. The matter is in the hands of the local police.

This letter is to give you notice that, should the police be unsuccessful in recovering the ring, I shall require to claim the full amount for which the ring is insured, namely, £200. I shall be glad to answer any further questions you may wish to put.

Yours faithfully,
JENNIFER STRATTON.

The Manager,
Regal Insurance Company,
Lombard Street, E.C.

EMPLOYMENT

No. 110.—From a Lady Inquiring for a Servant

THE CEDARS,
BURLEY, HANTS.

(*Date in full*).

DEAR SIR,

I need a competent cook-general to undertake the

running of my house, and understand you may be able to supply me with one. The house is a small one (four bedrooms) and the household consists only of myself and my husband, with occasional visits from our two daughters at Christmas, Easter, etc. We entertain a little—a small dinner party about once a week, say. A woman from the village comes to help with the rough work. Our previous cook-general was with us for twelve years. We provide a pleasant bed-sitting room with radio for the use of our resident servant. I trust that these particulars will enable you to send us someone suitable.

Yours faithfully,
ALICE MILBANKE.

To The Manager,
Queens Employment Agency,
777 Marylebone High Street, W.1.

No. 111.—From a Lady to a Prospective Mother's-Help

AMBERLEY,
HARRISON ROAD,
BUSHEY.

(*Date in full*).

DEAR MRS. ROBINSON,

Mrs. Sutherland, for whom I understand you work, has told me that you are free to undertake similar work elsewhere and suggested that you might suit me.

I need someone to help two or three mornings or afternoons—about eight hours a week in all, with perhaps some "baby-sitting" in the evenings by arrangement. The duties are general house-cleaning and some ironing; but I do want someone who would not mind taking charge of my two children occasionally if I have to be out, and perhaps cooking them a light lunch and taking them out for a walk. It is therefore essential that whoever comes to me should be fond of children and able to handle them well. Mrs. Sutherland has told me that you have looked after her boys on occasion.

If you can undertake this work, will you let me know? We can then discuss times of work, payment, and so forth. I am always at home in the morning, if you wish to call or telephone.

Yours faithfully,
MARY RUSHBROOKE.

No. 112.—Reply to above

17 CANON VILLAS,
BUSHEY.

(*Date in full*).

DEAR MADAM,

Thank you for your letter. I shall be pleased to work for you providing the payment and times you want me are suitable. I am fond of children so shall be happy to look after yours. I will call upon you on Thursday morning next to discuss the details.

Yours faithfully,
G. ROBINSON.

No. 113.—Request for Temporary Help

3 HILLSIDE DRIVE,
STOKE UNDERTON,
SOMERSET.

(*Date in full*).

DEAR MRS. LANGRIDGE,

Mrs. Sutherland has given me your name and told me you have helped her on occasion. I wonder if you could come to help me for a short period?

My husband's mother, who lives with us, is failing in health and confined to her room. As we are hoping to take a holiday next month, we need someone to take charge of the house and look after her while we are away. The old lady is quite independent as regards washing and dressing, etc., but needs someone to keep her room in order, make her bed, shop and prepare the meals and generally look after things. The ordinary work of the house is dealt with by a woman who comes in the mornings; we have quite a pleasant house with a big garden and television, and are a quarter of a mile from shops and buses.

If you are free to undertake this temporary position (we hope to be away for the first three weeks in August) will you let me know your terms? Then if it seems we can come to some arrangement, perhaps you would care to come over one day for a cup of tea so that I can show you the house and introduce you to my mother-in-law.

Yours faithfully,
ELIZABETH PARKER.

No. 114.—Reply to above

17 WEST WAY,
BRISTOL.

(*Date in full*).

DEAR MADAM,

Thank you for your letter. I am happy to say I am free to come for the three weeks of your holiday. My terms are six guineas a week with, of course, all found, plus fares incurred. If this is convenient to you, perhaps you will let me know.

I shall be glad to pay a preliminary visit as you suggest, but must ask you to refund my fares also on this occasion. If you are agreeable to this, will you let me know when you would like me to come.

Yours faithfully,
SARAH LANGRIDGE.

No. 115.—Application for Position as Nanny

13 SUSSEX STREET,
HARROW.

(*Date in full*).

DEAR MADAM,

I beg to apply for the position of nanny which you advertise.

My age is 33 and I received my training first as nursery maid in the Countess of Buckingham's nurseries and subsequently as under-nanny with the Hon. Mrs. George MacIntyre. For the past five years I have been working in a residential nursery run by the Middlesex County Council, but now desire to return to private employment. I am fully experienced, capable of taking sole charge, preparing the children's meals and looking after their clothes.

I can call upon you for a personal interview at any time.

Yours faithfully,
MIRIAM FOSTER.

No. 116.—Taking up a Reference

ROCKMOUNT,
MANOR PARK,
WELLINGTON.

(*Date in full*).

DEAR MADAM,

Miss Vera Glen has applied for a post as nanny with me and has given me your name as her last employer. I should be grateful for your opinion of her character and professional abilities, in confidence of course. Would you be kind enough to let me have a line as soon as convenient?

Yours truly,
GRACE NELSON.

No. 117.—Reply to above

(N.B. Reference to a servant's character is privileged in law; i.e., should it be necessary to say anything derogatory, no action for libel or slander can be taken, provided the comment is made in good faith and without malice.)

75 The Parade,
Southsea.

Dear Madam,

I am glad you think of employing Miss Vera Glen as your nanny; we are all very fond of her as she has been with us for six years and is only leaving because my youngest boy is now away at school. Miss Glen has a thorough knowledge of her duties and I found she had a pleasant knack of handling the children with the minimum of fuss and trouble. The nursery was always a happy place. One small difficulty was that she did not take kindly to being asked to undertake duties not strictly within her province; but perhaps this problem will not arise in your household. Apart from this minor criticism, I have nothing but praise for her.

Yours truly,
Agnes French.

No. 118.—Another—Unfavourable

75 The Parade,
Southsea.

Dear Madam,

In reply to your inquiry about Miss Glen, I regret that I cannot recommend her unreservedly. That she has a thorough theoretical knowledge of her job I must admit, and she is hard-working and efficient; but I found her rather too opinionated, unwilling to accept suggestions or advice, and at times actually rude. Furthermore she is not very adaptable and cannot vary her routine when necessary. But my real reason for parting with her was that the very strict nursery discipline she enforces has greatly upset my younger daughter who is affectionate and highly-strung.

I feel that Miss Glen is really more suited to an institutional post than a private family, although she has many good qualities.

Yours truly,
AGNES FRENCH.

No. 119.—General Reference for a Servant

To Whom It May Concern. Mrs. Annie Crosthwaite has been employed by me as cook-general for the past seven years and is leaving me only because, my household now being reduced in size, I have no need for her services. I have always found her a very industrious and capable worker, loyal and unselfish. She is completely honest and of very good character generally. She is capable of taking charge in an emergency and gets on well with other employees. I have much pleasure in recommending her.

No. 120.—Application for Employment in a Shop

50 CARLTON STREET,
LONDON, S.W.1.
(*Date in full*).

DEAR SIRS,

With reference to your advertisement for a young lady to manage the Millinery Department, I beg to apply for the position. I have been four years in the millinery department of Messrs. Cook & Co and during that time for two years attended evening classes in millinery and dress-making, at the Kensington Gore Evening Institute. I wish to make a change now as there seems no chance of promotion in my present post. I am 20 years old and was educated at St. Brendan's High School, having passed G.C.E. in English and Needlework.

I can call for an interview should you wish, and in the meantime enclose a testimonial from my former head-mistress. I would have to give a week's notice to terminate my present work. The matter of salary can be settled at an interview, if you feel my application suitable.

Yours faithfully,
ANGELA LEIGH.

No. 121.—Application for Employment as Hotel Maid

17 MAIN STREET,
LUTON.
(*Date in full*).

DEAR SIR,

I beg to apply for the situation advertised as vacant. My last employer was Mr. West of the White Hart Hotel. I left because of ill-health, but am now quite recovered. My age is 32. I give below the names and addresses of two people who have agreed to act as references.

Yours faithfully,
THERESA DELANEY.

No 122.—Application for Position as Secretary

40 ELDON ROAD,
LONDON, N.W.3.
(*Date in full*).

DEAR SIR,

With reference to your advertisement in the *Telegraph* this morning, I beg to apply for the position of secretary.

I have had 11 months experience in the firm of Taylor Watson Ltd., but now wish to leave there, for purely personal reasons. They will, I am sure, testify as to my qualifications and ability. I am eighteen years old, was educated at North Stoke Grammar School and took a commercial training at Stoke Technical College. My typing speed is —— words per minute, and my shorthand —— words per minute. I can call for an interview if you wish.

Yours faithfully,
DOROTHY ELLIS.

No. 123.—Another Application (general form)

14 PARIS ROAD,
LONDON, S.E.1.
(*Date in full*).

DEAR SIRS,

My friend Miss Hargreaves has informed me that you are looking out for a clerk (or secretary, typist, etc.) and has suggested that I should apply to you for the appointment. I am well accustomed to business, can write shorthand and type, and can work on my own initiative if required. Miss Hargreaves made no reference to salary but no doubt we can come to some agreement if you feel it worth while to grant me an interview.

Yours truly,
ROSE JACOBS.

No. 124.—Requesting a Reference on Appointment

4 NEAVER ROAD,
LONDON, N.11.
(*Date in full*).

DEAR MR. JONES,

I venture to write and ask if you have any objection to

be my reference as to character, etc.? I have the chance of an appointment with Messrs. Wilson, and have taken the liberty of mentioning your name as a reference to the firm. So, if they write, perhaps you will not mind saying what you know of me, as you have known me a good many years now.

Thanking you very much in anticipation of your kindness,

Yours sincerely,
KATHLEEN MAYER.

No. 125.—Requesting an Employer's Reference

16 HERBERT ROAD,
BRIGHTON.

(*Date in full*).

DEAR SIRS,

I wish to apply for a position with Imperial Chemical Industries and I should be greatly obliged if you would let me have a letter of recommendation.

I am in no way dissatisfied with my present position with you, and am applying for this post only because of the excellent prospects of promotion.

Yours faithfully,
JOHN HARGREAVES.

No. 126.—Application for Employment as Bookkeeper

23 BURTON ROAD,
LONDON, W.C.1.

(*Date in full*).

DEAR SIR,

In reply to your advertisement for a young lady to keep books at a family hotel, I wish to apply, as I am fully qualified for this work. I have been, for the past three years, doing the books of a large hotel in the country and attending to the business correspondence there. I left recently on account of a change in the management, but the present manager, as well as the former, have both agreed to act as references should you consider my application. My age is 27. I could begin work at once.

I enclose the names and addresses of the two gentlemen to whom I have referred.

Yours faithfully,
MARGARET KING.

No. 127.—From a Nurse at the Seaside about her Charges

MARINE SQUARE,
FRINTON.
(*Date in full*).

DEAR MRS. TAYLOR,

I am glad to be able to send a good report of the children this evening; they are all very happy and seem better already for the change. It has been a fine day and we have spent the whole of it on the sands, only coming indoors for meals. Mrs. Jones is kind and obliging and the cooking is good. I have just put the children to bed and told them I was about to write to you. They all send their love, and Miss Rosa particularly asks me to say she hopes you and the Master will be able to come down on Saturday.

I am,
Yours truly,
NURSE HALFORD.

No. 128.—From a Servant left in Charge of the House

75 Forest Road,
Hampstead, N.W.3.
(*Date in full*).

Dear Madam,

I hope you are having a good holiday and that Mr. Shaw and the children, as well as yourself, are well.

Everything is in order here, and I have got on well with the extra cleaning you asked me to do. I have to report, however, that on Tuesday morning there appeared to be some severe leakage from the overflow pipe of the tank in the roof. I knew you would not wish it left until your return, so I called in Mr. Green the plumber who was able to put matters right quite quickly. I trust this will meet with your approval.

Yours truly,
Gladys Dale.

No. 129.—From a Lady to a Servant in Charge

The Grand Hotel,
Swanage, Dorset.
(*Date in full*).

Dear Mary,

We intend to return next Thursday and shall travel by a train reaching London at 4 o'clock which will enable us to arrive home about half-past four. Will you please have tea ready for the children and the house in good order, being particularly careful to see that all the bedding is well aired. If it is a cold day, please light the fires. I leave it to you to prepare a plain dinner for Mr. Shaw and myself and you can tell the tradesmen to call again on Friday.

Yours sincerely,
Ethel Shaw.

LETTERS FROM PARENTS TO AND ABOUT THEIR CHILDREN

No. 130.—Inquiring about a School

"HILL CREST,"
17 HOPE ROAD,
LONDON, S.W.10.
(*Date in full*).

To the Headmaster,
St. George's School.

DEAR SIR,

My husband and I are facing the problem of educating our boy James and would like to discuss with you the possibility that he might become a pupil at St. George's. Would you be kind enough to send us a prospectus of the School and also let us know when it would be convenient for us to call upon you. Before finally arriving at any decision we would like to see the School for ourselves and know more about various points which really need personal discussion, such as the religious education that is given, what outside exams the children are prepared for, size of classes, and so forth.

I hope you will be able to see us within the next two or three weeks as we hope to get this matter of our boy's schooling decided well in advance of the start of the next autumn term.

Yours faithfully,
EDNA FITZGIBBON.

No. 131.—To a Headmistress about a Backward Pupil

CHERRY TREE COTTAGE,
WOOD LANE,
HATFIELD.

(*Date in full*).

DEAR MISS GRAY,

May I trespass upon your valuable time, to raise the subject of Caroline's studies, mathematics in particular? She has never found this subject easy and I fear she is rather slow, though careful and conscientious; and now that she is with Miss Brown for this subject, is finding things more difficult than ever. I am not implying any criticism of Miss Brown, whose teaching methods must of course be adapted to suit the class as a whole. Caroline does feel, however, that she is often hurried on from one point to the next before she has completely grasped each one, and I wonder if just a little more explanation from her teacher and care to see that each point is understood before passing on, might not make all the difference. Caroline does try and wants to succeed, so I feel she deserves sympathetic encouragement. I know you will understand.

I would much have preferred to discuss this matter personally with you and possibly with Miss Brown; unfortunately, however, I am unable to visit the School before half-term, by which date valuable time would have been lost. That is my reason for raising the matter now.

Yours sincerely,
MARY SINCLAIR.

No. 132.—Acknowledging the Award of a Scholarship

CHERRY TREE COTTAGE,
WOOD LANE,
HATFIELD.

(*Date in full*).

DEAR MISS GREY,

Thank you for your letter telling us of Caroline's success in winning a County Scholarship, of which we also received notice from the authorities by the same post.

I need hardly say how delighted we are. It is pleasant to know that the authorities feel Caroline is worth help and encouragement in the future. My husband and I would like to express our very sincere appreciation of the work of yourself and your staff at School, without which Caroline would not have had this success.

Yours sincerely,
MARY SINCLAIR.

No. 133.—From a Lady regarding her Daughter's Inattention at School

5 FULTON ROAD,
LONDON, N.10.

(*Date in full*).

DEAR MISS HUTCHINGS,

Thank you for your letter of yesterday; although it caused me great concern I am grateful to you for raising the matter of Elizabeth's behaviour at school.

Elizabeth has not been in the best of health lately as she has been growing fast and she has also been rather upset because her older sister, of whom she is very fond, has married and gone abroad. Altogether it has been an abnormal few months. I mention this not as an excuse for her conduct but because I think it gives us reason to hope that as her health and spirits improve, her conduct may do so too.

I have, however, had a serious talk with her, pointing out that time ill-spent now cannot be recovered and that she owes it to her teachers, and all who are fond of her, to control and discipline herself and try to work steadily. She has promised to try and do better and I trust that you will find an improvement in her from now on.

Yours sincerely,
MADGE FITZROY.

No. 134.—From a Mother to her Daughter at Boarding School, Remonstrating

7 CASTLETON ROAD,
ST. ALBANS.

(*Date in full*).

MY DEAR ELIZABETH,

I have had a letter from your headmistress in which she tells me that this term she and your other teachers have been very disappointed both in your general conduct and your school work. I know it has been an unsettling time for you, darling, and that you are growing fast and often feel tired. But every one of us has trials and a cross to bear—and this, for the moment, is yours. Daddy and I do hope that you will bear it bravely and not give way to naughtiness and laziness. We are proud of you and want you to be a credit to the family. Nobody expects impossibilities and we are not asking for perfection, but we do expect you to keep trying steadily. Then we know you will not only give satisfaction to your teachers, but life will be much happier and pleasanter for your yourself.

I wish we were nearer to you as it might help you to talk over your difficulties with Daddy or me. However, that cannot be for some time yet. But there is another source of strength open to all of us, and I feel sure that if you mention your difficulties in your prayers, and ask for help and guidance, it will be forthcoming.

Your loving
MOTHER.

No. 135.—Requesting for a Pupil to be Excused Lessons

CHERRY TREE COTTAGE,
WOOD LANE,
HATFIELD, HERTS.
(*Date in full*).

DEAR MISS GREY,

Would you kindly allow Caroline to leave school at 2.30 p.m. tomorrow instead of at the usual end of afternoon school? I have to take her to the dentist and was unable to make an appointment at any other time.

Yours sincerely,
MARY SINCLAIR.

No. 136.—Another

CHERRY TREE COTTAGE,
WOOD LANE,
HATFIELD.
(*Date in full*).

DEAR MISS GREY,

Caroline has had her eyes tested by the specialist at the Royal City Hospital and he says she needs special glasses. In the meantime, until they are ready, he thinks that she should not read or do close work. Would you, therefore, be kind enough to excuse her from such work at school for the time being? I hope she will be able to keep up with the class by listening to the lessons and that she can catch up on written work when she has her spectacles.

Yours sincerely,
MARY SINCLAIR.

MISCELLANEOUS

No. 137.—Letter of Apology

CRABTREE COTTAGE,
NEAR PETWORTH.
(*Date in full*).

DEAR MISS HARTINGFORD,

From our brief meeting yesterday and your remarks at that time, it is clear to me that I have been the unwitting cause of trouble and distress to you. To be truthful, I have felt for some time that everything was not right between us, but have been at a loss to know the reason. Now that the matter has been brought into the open, I feel that I owe you a very sincere apology for any action of mine that may have had results quite different from what I intended. Believe me, my only thought was to be helpful to yourself and other people, and if my good intentions went astray, I can but say that I am sorry.

Although it has made me sad to know that I have been the cause of trouble, I am only glad that the matter is cleared up at last and trust that we can now resume on the old footing. If at any time I can make amends in some material manner, I trust you will give me the chance to do so.

Yours very sincerely,
MARY NETHERFIELD.

No. 138.—Letter of Reference

5 King Street,
Oxbridge.

(*Date in full*).

Dear Miss Stephens,

In reply to your inquiry about Jane Verner, who has applied for membership of the Institute of Professional Painters in Water Colours, I am delighted to be able to recommend her unhesitatingly for membership. Miss Verner has high standards both of conduct and craftsmanship and great professional integrity. She was a most serious student when at college here. I have known Miss Verner and her family for ten years now and they are all greatly respected here. I feel sure that if you admit Miss Verner to membership she will be a most valuable member of the Institute.

Yours sincerely,
Marcia Anderson.

No. 139.—Letter to a Member of Parliament

7 Queen's Row,
Tamebridge.

(*Date in full*).

John Purdie, Esq., M.C., M.P.,
The House of Commons.

Dear Sir,

As one of your constituents, I wish to draw your attention to a matter which is likely to cause considerable hardship or worse, among families with young children.

As you probably know, there has for some years been an open-air children's playground at the corner of Westgate Road and Alamein Street, which has not only afforded opportunities for healthy outdoor activity to children in this very crowded area, but has also meant that mothers could safely leave their children there in the care of the attendant while they shopped in the nearby streets which, because of the extreme traffic congestion, are unsuitable for young children.

Now it appears that the playground is to be closed and the site used for, of all things, a cinema and a public house. An alternative playground is apparently planned, but it will be some years before this can be constructed and in any event, it is to be sited at the other end of Westgate Road, by the park, where it will be much less useful.

I have made representations to the Borough Council, but have received only a non-committal reply. In the interests of the children, whose safety and even lives depend upon having this protected place to play, I ask that you will take the matter up in the House of Commons to see if the Council's high-handed action can be stopped.

Yours faithfully,
ELSIE STIRLING.

No. 140.—Letter to a Local Councillor

57 PARK STREET,
UFFINGTON.

(*Date in full*).

To Councillor Mrs. Beddoes.

DEAR MADAM,

As a local government elector of Park Ward, I write on behalf of a number of local residents to put before you what we feel is a genuine grievance.

At a recent meeting of the Parent-Teacher Association of Uffington Primary school, the headmistress, Miss Fox, stated that it was not her policy to coach the children for the Eleven Plus exam. She gave reasons for this, which may be good in theory, but the fact remains that pupils from this school have, over some years, done less well in this vital exam than pupils from other local schools where preliminary coaching is given. Uffington Primary School children do not, in fact, get so many grammar school places as youngsters from other schools in the area.

As parents and ratepayers, we feel the council should have a uniform policy in this matter. Either coaching should be given at all schools, or at none, so that all children have an equal chance. I therefore ask you to raise the matter with the Education Committee at the next meeting. If you wish, I shall be pleased to arrange a small informal meeting of local ratepayers, so that we could explain our grievances more fully to you.

Yours sincerely,
JANE HENNEKEY.

SHIPPING AND EXPORT

No. 141.—Giving an Order for Goods

4 LOGAN STREET,
LIVERPOOL.

(*Date in full*).

(*Name and Address of Addressees*).

DEAR SIRS,

Please purchase for my account 200 bales fair Oomrawuttee cotton, at the market price, on receipt of this order, and ship by a vessel classed A1 at Lloyds, affecting insurance on the usual basis. For the amount of the invoice I authorize you to draw upon me at six months' sight, and either attach the documents of the shipment to the draft or draw against credits. Kindly advise in due course of the purchase.

Yours faithfully,
WILLIAM COATS.

(The documents of the shipment are the bills of lading, insurance policy, and, if the draft is sold to a bank, a letter of hypothecation. Credits are instruments granted by bankers authorizing merchants to draw upon them for a certain sum of money; it being understood that the drafts will be used only in *bona fide* operations.)

No. 142.—Executing the Order

5 Bush Row,
London, E.C.4.
(*Date in full*).

(*Name and Address of Addressee*).

Dear Sir,

We acknowledge with thanks receipt of your order of March 19, instructing us to purchase for your account 200 bales fair Oomrawuttee cotton, and we have pleasure in advising that we have executed the commission at — per candy, which is equivalent to — per lb., free on board. The quality of the staple selected is very good, and we have taken every precaution to secure you against disappointment when the shipment reaches your port. We have engaged freight in the *Dhuleep Singh*, now loading, and we anticipate advising you by next mail of her departure, and forwarding to you the accounts of the shipment.

The tendency of prices in our market is upward, and should advices from your port continue favourable we are confident a considerable advance will take place.

Yours faithfully,
Barlow Brothers.

(It is usual to advise a purchase by wire, in which case a copy of the telegram should be enclosed with the letter of advice.)

No. 143.—Transmitting Accounts of a Shipment

5 Bush Row,
London, E.C.4.

(*Date in full*).

(*Name and Address of Addressee*).

Dear Sir,

Further to our letter of March 30, we beg to advise having shipped for your account 200 bales cotton, per *Dhuleep Singh*, for Liverpool, the invoice of which, amounting to £4,300, we enclose. Against the shipment we have drawn for a like sum at six months' sight, in favour of the National Bank of India, attaching the shipping documents to the draft, which please protect on presentation.

Yours faithfully,
Barlow Brothers.

No. 144.—Requesting Information Regarding a Market

15 Ham Street,
London, E.C.2.

(*Name and Address of Addressees*).

Dear Sirs,

We should be grateful if you would advise us regarding the state of the market of Port-au-Prince. We are making this inquiry because of the demand for our products in other markets of the West Indies, and are willing to offer your friends our agency if there is a reasonable prospect of shipping advantageously. Our transactions would not be confined to our own goods, as we would operate in any commodity likely to realize a fair profit.

Yours faithfully,
Jones, Foster & Co.

No. 145.—Reporting Favourably

999 Fenchurch Street,
London, E.C.3.

(*Name and Address of Addressees*).

Dear Sirs,

In reply to your letter of June 3, we enclose an extract from our friends' advices, from which you will see that the market is in a very encouraging condition. The outturn of the hill produce has been much greater than the planters expected, and when this became known a substantial upward movement in European commodities took place. Stocks are low, and shipments inwards are by no means numerous. We are therefore in a position to offer you encouraging assurances should you offer our friends your agency.

Yours faithfully,
Robert Walker & Co.

No. 146.—Reporting Unfavourably

Port-au-Prince.
(*Date in full*).

(*Name and Address of Addressees*).

Dear Sirs,

In reply to your letter of June 3, we regret to report that the market of Port-au-Prince is in a very depressed condition, due to the failure of the hill crops and large-scale unemployment. We are well aware of the value of your agency, and perhaps at some future time, when the market has improved, you will allow us to accept your offer. In the meantime please accept our thanks for your proposal.

Yours faithfully,
Noble, Walker & Co.

No. 147.—Consigning Goods for Sale

15 HAM STREET,
LONDON, E.C.2.
(*Date in full*).

(*Name and Address of Addressees*).

DEAR SIRS,

Messrs. Robert Walker & Company have shown us a copy of their recent advices from Port-au-Prince in which you state that market prospects there are very encouraging. We therefore propose consigning to your care for sale, on our account, a shipment of Chintz, of about 1,500 pieces, and 10 cases of fancy goods, as a trial operation. We hope you will be able to give us a good account of this transaction.

Yours faithfully,
PRINCE, FOSTER & CO.

No. 148.—Advising the Dispatch of Goods to Shipping Agents

15 HAM STREET,
LONDON, E.C.2.
(*Date in full*).

(*Name and Address of Addressees*).

DEAR SIRS,

We have today forwarded to your care, per Carver & Co., 25 packages for shipment, per *Rustam*, to Port-au-Prince, consigned to Messrs. Noble, Walker & Co. Please send bills of lading and statement of shipping charges, etc. to us direct.

Yours faithfully,
PRINCE, FOSTER & CO.

Particulars of Shipment

1/15. 15 cases, 1,500 pieces chintz value £800.
16/25. 10 cases, 800 pieces fancy shirtings value £400.

No. 149.—Shipping Agents handling Bills of Lading

42 Tollens Street,
Liverpool.

(*Date in full*).

(*Name and Address of Addressees*).

Dear Sirs,

In accordance with your instructions we have shipped on your account 25 packages, per *Rustam*, from Liverpool to Port-au-Prince, the bills of lading for which are enclosed. We also enclose a statement of shipping charges amounting to £23 7s. 6d.

Yours faithfully,
Perkins Brothers.

No. 150.—Ordering Insurance to be Effected

15 Ham Street,
London, E.C.2.

(*Date in full*).

(*Name and Address of Addressee*).

Sir,

Please effect insurance against all risks for £1,500, on 25 packages shipped per *Rustam* from Liverpool to Port-au-Prince, consigned to Messrs. Noble, Walker & Co., on our account.

Particulars of the shipment are given below.

Yours faithfully,
(State particulars) Prince, Foster & Co.

No. 151.—Effecting Insurance

999 THREADNEEDLE STREET,
LONDON, E.C.2.
(*Date in full*).

(*Name and Address of Addressees*).

SIR,

In accordance with your wishes, I have effected insurance against all risks for £1,500 at—on your account, on 25 packages, per *Rustam* from Liverpool to Port-au-Prince. The policy will be forwarded to you in due course.

Yours faithfully,
JOHN WALLDEN.

No. 152.—Enclosing Draft drawn against Consignment

15 HAM STREET,
LONDON, E.C.2.
(*Date in full*).

Messrs. Robert Walker & Co.,
Fenchurch Street,
London, E.C.3.

DEAR SIRS,

We enclose Bills of Lading for 25 packages cottons, per *Rustam*, consigned to your agents Messrs. Noble, Walker & Co., Port-au-Prince, for sale on our account, and also an invoice for the shipment, amounting to £1,473 15s. As arranged with your representative we have drawn at three months' date for £1,105 6s. 3d., as an advance of three-fourths of the invoice, and now enclose the draft for acceptance, which kindly return to us in due course.

Yours faithfully,
PRINCE, FOSTER & CO.

No. 153.—Enclosing Acceptance

999 FENCHURCH STREET,
LONDON, E.C.3.
(*Date in full*).

(*Name and Address of Addressees*).

DEAR SIRS,

We acknowledge with thanks receipt of your letter of yesterday, enclosing shipping documents per *Rustam* and draft amounting to £1,105 6s. 3d. for our acceptance as advance against shipment. We have pleasure in enclosing these duly honoured. We hope that the result of your venture will be sufficiently encouraging to induce you to ship at regular periods to our friends at Port-au-Prince.

Yours faithfully,
ROBERT WALKER & CO.

No. 154.—Transmitting Account Sales

PORT-AU-PRINCE.
(*Date in full*).

(*Name and Address of Addressees*).

DEAR SIRS,

We have pleasure in forwarding an account sales for 25 packages cotton per *Rustam*, net proceeds £1,780 14s., which we hope you will find correct. We are remitting this sum to our agents, Messrs. Robert Walker & Co., of London, who will render you an account and place the credit balance at your disposal. The result of the shipment has not been so large as we anticipated, owing to a falling off in the demand for piece goods soon after the arrival of the *Rustam*, but prices have not fallen below the level at which they were last season, and we confidently expect they will advance steadily as the up-country produce comes into the market. We prefer, however, to sell when a margin of profit can be obtained, rather than hold over goods in the hope of an advance, and we have dealt with your shipment as we deal with our own purchases.

Yours faithfully,
NOBLE, WALKER & CO.

No. 155.—Rendering an Account Current

999 FENCHURCH STREET,
LONDON, E.C.3.
(*Date in full*).

(*Name and Address of Addressees*).

DEAR SIRS,

Enclosed you will find a copy of account current for your shipment per *Rustam*, showing a balance of £403 9s. in your favour, together with a cheque for that sum. An Acknowledgement in due course will oblige.

Yours faithfully,
ROBERT WALKER & CO.

No. 156.—Reproaching Consignees for Poor Results

99 FORE STREET,
LONDON, E.C.2.
(*Date in full*).

(*Name and Address of Addressees*).

DEAR SIRS,

In acknowledging receipt of your letter of November 20, enclosing an account sales for my shipment per *Matheran*, I regret to say that the result is very disappointing. Relying upon the assurances of your agents on this side that the utmost attention would be paid to my interests,

I selected and shipped only such goods as were perfectly sound and in demand in your market. From your own advices I understood that the shipment was likely to arrive before the up-country buyers had completed their purchases, and that were the *Matheran* to arrive late, the local demand would be sufficient to take off my goods at figures which would leave a profit. In consequence, I expected a result very different from that which your account shows. In the circumstances, therefore, I think an explanation is due to me of the cause which led you to dispose of my goods at what I consider a sacrifice, seeing that the prices obtained were considerably below those reported as ruling in the market at the time the sales were made.

Regretting the necessity of addressing you in this manner,

Yours faithfully,
WILLIAM BLACK.

No. 157.—Explanatory Letter

PORT NATAL.

(*Date in full*).

(*Name and Address of Addressee*).

DEAR SIR,

In reply to your letter of December 2, requiring an explanation as regards the disposal of your shipment per *Matheran*, we can assure you that, had it not been for the absence of our manager at the time your account sales were transmitted, you would have been informed fully on the subject. Until your letter reached us, we were not aware that our assistant in charge had omitted to do this, and we offer our profound apologies for his unpardonable neglect.

Your shipment, we regret to say, arrived damaged partly by mildew and partly by sea-water, as you will gather from the enclosed survey certificate, and we felt bound to dispose of every package immediately by auction, as the best course to adopt in the circumstances. If the mildew was caused by the materials used by the manufacturer in producing the goods, you should claim compensation for loss from him. As regards the packages damaged by sea-water: your insurance policy was effected F.P.A. (free of particular average) and there is no claim on it. To enable you to establish your claims against the manufacturer, we enclose a certified copy of the auction sales and the depositions of several reputable buyers who examined the goods at the sale rooms.

We regret so much the result of the consignment that we have credited your account with £43 4s., the sum charged as commission in the account sales. Trusting you may be successful in obtaining compensation.

Yours faithfully,
BURNS, JONES & SON.

No. 158.—Instructing Agent to pass Goods through the Customs House

28 PRINCE'S STREET,
CLIFTON.

(*Date in full*).

(*Name and Address of Addressee*).

DEAR SIR,

The *Viceroy*, which arrived at your port yesterday from Calcutta, brought four cases to my address. Please pass these through the Customs House and forward them to me by rail at your earliest convenience.

The enclosed invoice shows the nature and value of the contents.

Yours faithfully,
ROBERT HENNIG.

No. 159.—Advice of Goods being Shipped

42 Richmond Road,
Bristol.

(*Date in full*).

(*Name and Address of Addressees*).

Dear Sirs,

We acknowledge with thanks receipt of your order of April 27, and in accordance with your instructions have shipped on board the *Rob Roy*, for your account and risk, 10 packages as per invoice enclosed.

We hope that the goods will arrive in a sound condition and will give you satisfaction. A few articles, which from their novelty and quality ought to find a good market in your city, have been added.

Yours faithfully,
Clyde, Howe & Co.

No. 160.—Reply to a Letter advising the Arrival of a Shipment

David House,
Exchange,
Glasgow.

(*Date in full*).

(*Name and Address of Addressees*).

Dear Sirs,

I have your letter of February 15, and am happy to hear that the goods per the *Robert Bruce* arrived safely.

I have duly honoured your bill for £200, due on the 10th.

On receipt of the silk per the *Queen of Burmah* I will write again, and will obtain the best price possible.

Yours faithfully,
David Stirling.

No. 161.—Drawing and Manner of Reimbursement

1,000 TOOLEY STREET,
LONDON, S.E.1.
(*Date in full*).

(*Name and Address of Addressees*).

DEAR SIRS,

We wish to accredit our friends Messrs. Galt & Co. of Stockholm on your good house for the sum of £1,000. It will, however, depend on circumstances whether they will avail themselves of this, but if they do so please confirm it of them. For your reimbursement you may draw on us for the amount at the most favourable rate of exchange obtainable. In view of our former relations, we are sure that you will readily grant us this facility, and we trust it will lead to more extensive business between us.

Yours faithfully,
GLENN, JAMES & CO.

No. 162.—Regarding the above Draft and Confirming a Credit

HAMBURG.
(*Date in full*).

(*Name and Address of Addressees*).

DEAR SIRS,

We have received the enclosed copy letter from our friends, Messrs. Glen, James & Co. of London, with a request to forward it to you and at the same time confirm the credit for £1,000 sterling, which these gentlemen advise to have opened with us in your favour. We have the honour of assuring you that your drafts for this amount for account of our mutual friends will be duly protected.

Yours faithfully,
LEO & CO.

No. 163.—Advice of a Draft

STOCKHOLM.

(*Date in full*).

(*Name and Address of Addressees*).

DEAR SIRS,

We have received from Messrs. Leo and Co. of Hamburg a confirmation of the credit you have been kind enough to open with them in our favour, and we wish to advise that we have today drawn on our mutual friends for £850, which we are sure will receive due protection. As our transactions with you have ceased for this year, please place that sum against the net proceeds of our consignment of tallow per *Stockholm.* At the end of three months we shall take the liberty of drawing for the remainder direct on your goodselves, if this is agreeable to you.

Yours faithfully,

GALT & CO.

No. 164.—Executing part of an Order and drawing for the Amount

44 FELLOW STREET,
GLASGOW.

(*Date in full*).

(*Name and Address of Addressees*).

DEAR SIRS,

We refer you to our letter of May 1, advising the execution of part of your order. Unfortunately, owing to the present political crisis in Europe there has been a severe hardening on our prices, and we find it impossible to purchase the remainder. We are pleased that the change which must consequently take place in your market will enable you to profit considerably by this shipment, and induce you to favour us again with your orders.

The invoice amount, £1,462 5s., has been placed to your debit, and our drafts on Hamburg balance this sum. We have today sent the bill of lading to Bremen and the insurance policy to Amsterdam.

Yours faithfully,
GLENTIES, TODD & CO.

No. 165.—Introducing the Captain of a Ship

1,000 FENCHURCH STREET,
LONDON, E.C.3.
(*Date in full*).

(*Name and Address of Addressee*).

DEAR SIR,

This is to introduce to you Captain Jennings of the *Dharwar*, who is about to depart with his ship to Bombay. If you will give Captain Jennings any assistance in your power and help him to obtain a speedy discharge and good return freight, I shall be greatly obliged.

Thanking you in anticipation of your services.

Yours faithfully,
HENRY BLUNT.

LETTER-WRITER FOR GENTLEMEN

LETTER-WRITER FOR GENTLEMEN

INVITATIONS

No. 1.—Invitation to Dinner

Mr. and Mrs. Green request the pleasure of Mr. Fisher's company at dinner on Wednesday, June 13th at 7.30 o'clock.

4 York Terrace,
S.W.18.
(*Date in full*).

No. 2.—Reply to above

Mr. Maurice Fisher accepts with much pleasure Mr. and Mrs. Green's kind invitation to dinner on Wednesday, June 13th.

Lime Cottage,
S.W.18.
(*Date in full*).

No. 3.—Another reply, declining

Mr. Maurice Fisher regrets that a previous engagement prevents him from accepting Mr. and Mrs. Green's kind invitation to dinner on Wednesday, June 13th.

No. 4.—Invitation, less formal

999 PICCADILLY,
LONDON, W.1.
(*Date in full*).

MY DEAR CHARLES,

Thomas Wilson and a few other friends are dining with me on Tuesday the 17th at 7.30 for 8 o'clock. Can you join us? As most people will be coming straight from their offices, we're not dressing.

Yours sincerely,
WALTER SIMSON.

No. 5.—Reply to above

CARLTON CLUB,
LONDON, S.W.1.
(*Date in full*).

DEAR WALTER,

Thank you for your invitation for Tuesday the 17th, which I accept with pleasure. I shall greatly look forward to seeing Tom Wilson again; it is some time since we met.

Yours sincerely,
CHARLES MUNRO.

No. 6.—Another reply, declining

CARLTON CLUB,
LONDON, S.W.1.
(*Date in full*).

DEAR WALTER,

Thank you for your kind invitation for the 17th. I am sorry to say, however, that I shall be unable to come, as I shall be out of town on business during the early part of that week. Please remember me to Tom Wilson—I am particularly sorry to miss this chance of renewing acquaintance with him.

Yours sincerely,
CHARLES MUNRO.

No. 7.—Invitation to lunch at a Restaurant

18 BERKELEY COURT,
LONDON, W.1.
(*Date in full*).

DEAR DAVID,

Can you have lunch with me one day next week? There are one or two matters I should very much like to talk over with you and upon which I should value your opinion. Would Wednesday suit you? If so, I suggest the Rumania Restaurant at 1 o'clock. Let me know if this will be convenient and I will book a table.

Yours sincerely,
JAMES HOLLAND.

No. 8.—Reply accepting

400 ST. JAMES'S SQUARE,
LONDON, W.1.
(*Date in full*).

DEAR JAMES,

I shall be delighted to lunch with you on Wednesday and the time and place you suggest will suit me excellently. I look forward to seeing you then.

Yours sincerely,
DAVID PARKER.

No. 9.—Reply declining

400 St. James's Square,
London, W.1.
(*Date in full*).

Dear James,

I should very much like to lunch with you on Wednesday but am already booked for that day. Thursday or Friday are all right for me however; would you care to make it one of those days?

Yours,
David Parker.

No. 10.—Invitation to a Lady to Lunch

5 Lancaster Road,
W.1.
(*Date in full*).

Dear Jane,

If you are free on Wednesday and have nothing better to do, I wonder if you would care to have lunch with me? I suggest the Ruritania Restaurant at 1 o'clock—they have some rather good foreign food there. I look forward to hearing whether you are able to come.

Yours,
John Stebbings.

No. 11.—Formal Invitation to a Wedding

Invitations for weddings are printed or engraved, the name of the recipient being written in by hand; good stationers will show samples of the kind of thing that is usual.

Mr. and Mrs. Henry Sherwood
Request the pleasure of the company of
Mr. John Thompson
on the occasion of
the marriage of their daughter
Joan Christine
to
Captain Peter Cholmondeley
at St. John's Church, W.1. at 2.30 p.m.
and afterwards at
The Barchester Hotel.

R.S.V.P. to
999 Hyde Park Gardens, W.2.

No. 12.—Acceptance

21 Russell Court,
W.1.

(*Date in full*).

Mr. John Thompson has much pleasure in accepting Mr. and Mrs. Henry Sherwood's kind invitation to the marriage of their daughter Joan Christine on Monday, June 8th.

No. 13.—Declining above

21 Russell Court,
W.1.

(*Date in full*).

Mr. John Thompson much regrets that he is unable to accept Mr. and Mrs. Sherwood's kind invitation to the marriage of their daughter on June 8th, as he will be out of town.

No. 14.—Formal Invitation to an At Home

These are usually printed, the name of the recipient being written in. Special cards can be bought from most stationers with spaces for the filling in of details of time and place. The form is as follows:

Mrs. James Robinson
AT HOME
Monday, June 10th
4 p.m.—6 p.m.

19 John Street,
Hampstead, N.W.3. R.S.V.P.

No. 15.—Acceptance of above

Acceptance or refusal should be formal, as in the case of wedding invitations, e.g.:

Mr. Allan Gerrard has much pleasure in accepting the invitation of Mrs. James Robinson for Monday, June 10th at 4 p.m.

11 Dale Road, N.W.3.

No. 16.—Formal Invitations to Dances, Bridge Parties, Garden Parties and Similar Functions

These follow the form of At Home invitations, the word "Dancing", "Bridge", etc., being added in the left hand bottom corner. The forms of acceptance and refusal are as for wedding invitations.

No. 17.—Invitation to Official Function

The President and Council
of the
Greater London Hellenic Arts Society
request the pleasure of the company of
Mr. Philip Brocklehurst
at a Reception
at Burlingham House, W.1.
on Thursday, 5th October at 5.30 p.m.
to mark the centenary of the Society's Foundation.

R.S.V.P. to
199 Greek Street,
W.1.

Dress Informal.

No. 18.—Acceptance of above

987 FROGNAL RISE,
N.W.3.

(*Date in full*).

Mr. Philip Brocklehurst thanks the President and Council of the Greater London Hellenic Arts Society for their invitation to a Reception on 5th October to mark the centenary of the Society's Foundation, and has pleasure in accepting.

No. 19.—Letter of Thanks for an Evening's Entertainment

9 ULVERSTONE RISE,
WIMBLEDON.

(*Date in full*).

DEAR MRS. BARING,

Thank you so much for a delightful evening yesterday. It was a very great pleasure to walk in your lovely garden before dinner. And what a dinner! Please pass on my compliments to your cook; I don't know when I have tasted a more delicious soufflé. Thank you, again, for a really enjoyable evening.

Yours sincerely,
REX HALLIBURTON.

No. 20.—Invitation to Stay

27 QUEEN'S ROAD,
GODALMING.

(*Date in full*).

DEAR BRUCE,

If you are free, would you care to visit us the weekend after next? That is, from the 15th—17th September. The country is looking very fine just now and we can get some cub-hunting. Let me know if I may expect you.

Yours,
PETER EVANS.

No. 21.—Reply to above

17 LAKE ROAD,
CANONBURY.

(*Date in full*).

MY DEAR PETER,

Thank you for asking me down from 15th—17th September, and I am greatly looking forward to coming. I will travel down by the 10.20 train, but please do not trouble to meet it; I can easily make my own way from the station. The prospect of cub-hunting is rather exciting as this is something I have not done before.

Please remember me to your wife and the boys.

Yours sincerely,
BRUCE BANCROFT.

No. 22.—Another, declining

17 LAKE ROAD,
CANONBURY.

(*Date in full*).

DEAR PETER,

Thank you for your letter and kind invitation to stay. Unfortunately I am on duty that weekend and shall not be able to get away, which is a great disappointment. It would have been very nice to see you all again, and get a breath of country air in this lovely autumn weather.

With kind regards to Mrs. Evans and the boys.

Yours sincerely,
BRUCE BANCROFT.

No. 23.—Letter of Thanks for a Visit

17 LAKE ROAD,
CANONBURY.

(*Date in full*).

DEAR MRS. EVANS,

I arrived back last evening after quite a speedy and pleasant train journey. The carriage never got too crowded and we were in well on time.

I did so much enjoy my stay with you, and it was grand to see the boys again. How they are growing! It was awfully kind of them and Peter to take me cub-hunting, an experience I shall remember for a long long time. Thank you very much indeed for a lovely weekend.

Yours very sincerely,
BRUCE BANCROFT.

No. 24.—Invitation to go on a Motor Tour

HOLLOWBURY,
WARWICK.

(*Date in full*).

DEAR PETER,

Henry and I have decided to spend our holidays touring France in his car and as we shall have a spare seat, wondered whether you would care to join us.

Our plan at the moment is to start on the 15th June and go via Paris, where we shall probably look up some old friends, and then down through the wine country and to the Mediterranean by easy stages. Although we expect to be able to get hotel accommodation without advance booking, we shall take camping equipment so that we can be independent of hotels if we feel like it. We haven't yet planned an exact route or timetable; perhaps you have some suggestions to contribute?

As we shall be making an early start on the 15th, could you come and stay the night here on the 14th?

Expenses we should, of course, be sharing, pooling cost of petrol, meals, etc. Henry says he can't afford more than £30 and nor can I, so if you feel the same, we shall just have as good a time as we can until the money begins to run out, then head for home.

If this sounds interesting to you, let me know. We both hope you can join us.

Yours ever,
MICHAEL.

No. 25.—Reply to above

THE HIGHLANDS,
NR. LANCASTER.
(*Date in full*).

DEAR MICHAEL,

I like the sound of your proposed holiday and shall be very pleased to join you and Henry. I'll have to see my chief and make sure it is all right for me to take my holiday then, but I don't anticipate any difficulty on that score—most of the other chaps in the department are fathers of families who all want their holidays in August. And I should think I could raise £30 for my share of the cost. So barring accidents I will join you on the 14th as you suggest.

Many thanks for asking me
Yours,
PETER.

No.26.—Another, declining

THE HIGHLANDS,
NR. LANCASTER.
(*Date in full*).

DEAR MICHAEL,

I much appreciate your asking me to join you and Henry on holiday but I'm sorry to say it is out of the question for me this year. My Finals come at the end of July and I feel I really must stay at home and swot; as you'll appreciate it is fairly important to me to pass as well as possible, and work at the office has been so heavy during the past months I have fallen rather behind with my own studies. A pity, but there it is! I do hope you will both have a good holiday.

Yours always,
PETER.

No. 27.—Invitation to be a Godparent

"HOLMWOOD",
RIDGE HILL,
EPPING.

(*Date in full*).

MY DEAR JAMES,

Our son is now two weeks old and we are thinking about his baptism which I gather should take place next month. Helen and I would be so very honoured if you would be one of his godfathers. (My brother will be the other.)

If you feel able to undertake this, we thought of having the christening at St. Mark's Church, Elm Road (where we were married) on Sunday the 12th at 3 o'clock. Will you let me know if this day is convenient for you? Helen is planning some kind of tea-party at home afterwards.

Yours sincerely,
CHARLES SANDERSON.

No. 28.—Intimation of a funeral

" MON REPOS",
FERNLEA ROAD,
TAUNTON.

(*Date in full*).

DEAR MR. WILKINSON,

The funeral arrangements for my late uncle are as follows: the cortege leaves the house on Friday afternoon at 2 o'clock and arrives at St. John's Church at 2.15 for a short service before proceeding to the cemetery. I am letting you know this in case you or some other member of the firm may wish to be present.

Yours truly,
SIDNEY CARRON.

ANNOUNCEMENTS, LETTERS OF CONGRATULATION AND CONDOLENCE

No. 29.—Announcing a Birth (Insertion in Periodical)

Westcott. On May 17th, to Eileen (nee Smith) wife of George Westcott of 22 Chester Road, Brighton, a son, Timothy, brother for Jennifer and Susan.

No. 30.—Letter Announcing a Birth

22 CHESTER ROAD,
BRIGHTON.
(*Date in full*).

DEAR JOHN,

I know you will be pleased to hear that Eileen has a beautiful boy, born at 8.30 this morning.

With all good wishes,
Yours sincerely,
GEORGE WESTCOTT.

No. 31.—Announcing a Death

PARK HOUSE,
WESTFIELD, SURREY.
(*Date in full*).

DEAR MR. AND MRS. GIBBS,

I know you will be sorry to learn that my dear mother passed away this morning at daybreak.

Despite her long illness which ought to have prepared us for this, it comes upon us as a severe shock.

Yours sincerely,
HAROLD BILSTON.

No. 32.—Congratulations upon the Birth of a Child

THE HURST,
HORNSEY, N.8.
(*Date in full*).

MY DEAR ARTHUR,

Heartiest congratulations upon the birth of your son. You must both be extremely happy. I trust the baby is thriving and your wife having a satisfactory convalescence. I can only say that I hope your boy will bring you both as much happiness as our own children have done to Mary and myself.

Please convey my congratulations and good wishes to your wife when you see her. And Mary asks me to say that if you have an evening free when you are not visiting the hospital, do drop in and take pot-luck with us. We shall be so pleased to see you, and I know Mary is agog to hear all the details of the baby's weight and so forth.

Yours ever,
GEORGE FIELDING.

No. 33.—Another, ditto

17 DEVONSHIRE ROAD,
HOLLAND PARK, W.8.
(*Date in full*).

MY DEAR ALICE,

Please accept my sincere congratulations to you and Arthur upon the birth of a son. It was the one thing needed to complete your lives together. As an old bachelor, I realise strongly how much the world owes to the parents of beautiful children—without them it would be about as gay as a garden without flowers! Your little son will, I feel sure, bring you ever-increasing happiness in the years ahead.

I am delighted to hear from your mother that you are both getting on so well.

I am
Your boy's proud Great Uncle
HAROLD.

No. 34.—Congratulations upon a Son's Success

RYMOUNT,
CLISSOLD PARK, N.16.
(*Date in full*).

DEAR HENRY,

Allow me to congratulate you upon Ned's passing his final Law Society exam, which I read in the paper this morning. You must all be glad that his time of study and anxiety is over. It is most satisfactory when a son repays by hard work and success all the trouble and care that parents have put into his education. No doubt he will soon be made a junior partner. If at any time I can be of help in advancing his career, I trust you will give me the pleasure of allowing me to do so.

Yours very sincerely,
JAMES CARNABY.

No. 35.—Congratulations upon a Professional Success

4 MAY STREET,
LONDON, W.C.2.
(*Date in full*).

DEAR ROBIN,

It was with great pleasure that I read in the paper this morning of your appointment as Actuary and General Manager of the Manchester Merchants Life Insurance Company. This is an achievement indeed, but not more than you deserve. It is good to know that recognition has come your way so quickly. I trust that this appointment will give you even greater scope for both service to your profession and personal achievement. Please accept my heartiest congratulations and best wishes for the future.

Yours very sincerely,
JOHN DYSON.

No. 36.—Congratulations upon an Honour

5 VICARAGE ROAD,
PINNER, MIDDLESEX.
(*Date in full*).

MY DEAR JENKINSON,

Please accept my very sincere congratulations upon receiving the award of an M.B.E. in the New Year Honours, which I saw in this morning's paper. I know that your work, in itself, is far more important to you than any recognition you may gain by it. However, it is good to know that your efforts have not gone unrecorded and that merit has had its reward. My wife joins with me in sending our warmest congratulations on this well-merited honour, and very best wishes for the future.

Yours very sincerely,
FULKE GREENFORD.

No. 37.—Letter of Condolence

THE WILLOWS,
HATFIELD ROAD,
BARNET.
(*Date in full*).

DEAR MRS. BLUNDELL,

We were greatly shocked this morning at seeing the announcement of your father's death in the paper. We had heard he was ill but had no idea matters were so serious.

Please accept this expression of our heartfelt sympathy and regret for your loss. Your father had so many friends, and so endeared himself to us and everyone by his many unobtrusive kindnesses, that we feel we too have lost a great friend.

We all sympathise very deeply with you and pray that you may be sustained in this time of trial.

Believe me,
Yours very sincerely,
FREDERICK BROMSGROVE.

No. 38.—Another, Official

TURNER, ROBBINS & CO.,
BANBURY ROAD,
READING.

(*Date in full*).

DEAR MRS. HOWARD,

It was with a sense of shock and real sorrow that I learned of the death of your husband, and I know that these feelings are shared by all who knew him and worked with him during his years with this firm. Please accept this expression of heartfelt sympathy on behalf of his former colleagues here and of myself personally.

If there is anything at all that my colleagues and myself can do to lighten your present heavy burden, we should feel privileged to do so and we trust that you will not hesitate to apply to us if at any time we can be of service.

With every kind wish for yourself and family

Believe me
Yours truly,
JOHN TURNER.
(Chairman).

No. 39.—Condolence, More Distant

200 CHARLES STREET,
HOVE, SUSSEX.
(*Date in full*).

DEAR MRS. BROWN,

It was with deep regret that I heard of your bereavement, and I hope you will accept very sincere condolences at this sad time.

Mr. Brown will indeed be missed by all who were privileged to know him, for he did so much good both in his public work on the Council and as a private citizen and friend and benefactor to so many.

May I express, on behalf of my wife and myself, our very deep sympathy with you and your family.

Yours truly,
GEORGE SCRUTTON.

No. 40.—Condolence on the Death of a Wife or Child

THE DELL,
NORWOOD, S.W.23.
(*Date in full*).

MY DEAR MICHAEL,

Please accept my sincerest sympathy in your great loss. Nothing that one can say can adequately express the feelings of your friends, in the face of what you are going through. Elizabeth was greatly loved by us all and we sincerely mourn her loss, and remember with gratitude the radiance that she spread around her during her too-brief life.

Trusting that time may help to heal the terrible grief you are feeling, and praying that you may be sustained at this sad time.

I am,
With sincerest sympathy,
Your friend
ARTHUR FRANKLIN.

No. 41.—Reply to Letter of Condolence

HAMILTON VILLA,
GORING ON THAMES.
(*Date in full*).

MY DEAR ARTHUR,

At this time of sorrow it is a great help to know that friends are thinking of one. I still feel completely stunned and bewildered, and can hardly believe she has really gone. I cannot write more just now. But the thoughts and prayers of friends are a source of strength indeed.

Yours sincerely,
MICHAEL BOWERS.

No. 42.—Another, ditto

307 PORTMAN GARDENS,
LONDON, W.1.
(*Date in full*).

DEAR MR. BROMSGROVE,

Thank you for your kind letter. My father's passing has been a sad blow to us all, but it was not entirely unexpected; and we find consolation in the thought that he had a long and full life and in knowing, also, that so many friends are thinking of us with sympathy.

Yours sincerely,
JOHN BULLEN.

No. 43.—Another, ditto

7 MARYLEBONE SQUARE,
W.1.

(*Date in full*).

DEAR MR. TURNER,

Thank you for your letter on behalf of yourself and the firm. We still feel rather stunned by my father's passing. I am glad to say his illness was of short duration and he did not suffer. He would have been pleased to know that his former colleagues remembered him—he so often spoke of his days with the firm, as being a very happy period of his life.

It is most kind of you to inquire if we need help. As far as I can tell at the moment, my father seems to have settled his affairs very satisfactorily, but there are one or two matters upon which I should very much value your advice, or that of some member of the firm more versed in business affairs than myself. May I take advantage of your kind offer, and telephone your secretary for an appointment in, say, a week's time?

On behalf of my mother and myself, thank you again for your kind expression of sympathy.

Yours truly,
JOHN HOWARD.

REQUESTS, WITH REPLIES

No. 44.—Soliciting the Loan of Money from a Friend

MARINE VILLA,
BEACH ROAD,
LYME REGIS.
(*Date in full*).

MY DEAR EDWARD,

I have hesitated long before beginning this letter, for it is not going to be an easy one to write. You have known me, I think, long enough to know that it is not my habit to ask favours, especially financial ones. But an unexpected difficulty has arisen which obliges me to ask for your help. If you could see your way to lend me £100 for about six months' time, when I can confidently promise to repay it in full, it would be of inestimable help to me. If, however, I am asking something that is difficult or inconvenient, please forget the whole matter, for I would not on any account wish to trouble you unduly. Perhaps I ought to mention that before turning to you I have tried other channels but I regret to say without success. I need hardly say how sorry I am that it should have been necessary to approach you in this way.

Yours truly,
BRIAN MARSHALL.

No. 45.—Reply, Affirmatively

THE CLOISTERS,
HAVANT.

(*Date in full*).

DEAR MARSHALL,

I could not for one moment hesitate in answering your letter and enclose a cheque for the amount you need. As to repayment, please believe I shall not look for it until you have got over your troubles. I am sorry you did not apply to me in the first instance.

With every good wish,
Yours sincerely,
EDWARD GRAHAM.

No. 46.—Another reply, Refusing

THE CLOISTERS,
HAVANT.

(*Date in full*).

DEAR MARSHALL,

I am sorry to be unable to help you. My own affairs just now make it impossible for me conveniently to comply with your request. I sincerely trust that things will soon take a turn for the better with you.

Yours truly,
EDWARD GRAHAM.

No. 47.—To a Lady, Refusing Assistance

TEMPLE CHAMBERS,
LONDON, E.C.4.

(*Date in full*).

DEAR MADAM (OR, DEAR MISS BROWN),

In reply to your letter, I regret that it is not in my power to render the assistance for which you ask.

In reply to your letter of yesterday, I regret that it is not in my power to render the assistance for which you ask.

I will certainly let you know if I should hear of any vacancy in the type of work for which you are qualified. Unfortunately I can do nothing more, other than express my sincere wish that things will soon take a turn for the better in your affairs.

Yours faithfully,
ERNEST LOCKYER.

No. 48.—Requesting an Introduction to an Acquaintance

10 THE GARDENS,
SYDENHAM, S.E.26.
(*Date in full*).

DEAR MR. STANLEY,

Since our conversation the other day, things have taken a turn which will involve me in a visit to Birmingham very shortly. I wonder if you would be so kind as to give me a letter of introduction to the friend of whom you were speaking? I should esteem it a great favour.

Yours sincerely,
FREDERICK JONES.

No. 49.—Letter of Introduction

HURST MANOR,
LANGLEY MOOR.
(*Date in full*).

DEAR MR. CARTER,

The bearer of this letter, Mr. Frederick Jones, is a young friend of mine who is visiting your city on business.

Anything you can do to help him will be a kindness much appreciated by him and, I need hardly say, by me.

Yours sincerely,
WILFRED STANLEY.

No. 50.—Reply to above

"YEOMANS LODGE,"
BARNET GREEN.
(*Date in full*).

DEAR MR. STANLEY,

Mr. Jones called upon me yesterday with your letter, and we had a long and interesting talk. He strikes me as a young man who will go far! I have been able to help him to meet one or two people who may be useful and we expect him out here to dine on Thursday.

Yours sincerely,
FRANCIS CARTER.

No. 51.—Thanks for Letter of Introduction

MERCIA HOTEL,
BIRMINGHAM.
(*Date in full*).

DEAR MR. STANLEY,

I have to thank you again for the introduction you so kindly gave me to Mr. Francis Carter. He gave me a warm welcome and was unstinting of his time and advice; also, he very kindly put me in touch with some important men in my line of business.

I really am exceedingly obliged.

Yours very sincerely,
FREDERICK JONES.

No. 52.—Letter of Thanks for Kindness to a Friend

HURST MANOR,
LANGLEY MOOR.
(*Date in full*).

DEAR MR. CARTER,

I have to thank you very sincerely for your kind reception of young Jones. I thought you would find him interesting; his views on business are certainly stimulating! He tells me his trip has been both pleasant and very successful, principally due to your help. I appreciate it very much.

Yours sincerely,
WILFRED STANLEY.

No. 53.—Requesting Patronage of a Fund-raising Effort

THE WARREN,
RUSTINGTON PEVEREL,
BERKSHIRE.
(*Date in full*).

MY LORD (OR, DEAR SIR, OR, MADAM),

On behalf of the Rustington Peverel Community Association, may I beg the favour of your (Lordship's) patronage of our forthcoming Fête and Sale of Work on June 11th. It is to be held in an effort to raise funds for the building of a new wing for the Social Centre in the village. This institution, which has been established several years, is greatly in need of increased accommodation, owing to the large number of new residents in the satellite town being developed adjoining the village. I beg to enclose a copy of the last Annual Report, which describes in detail the very excellent work of the Social Centre.

The Committee is most anxious to make a real success of the Fête on June 11th, and if your Lordship will allow us to include your name as a Patron, the Committee will feel much honoured and greatly indebted.

I have the honour to be
Your Lordship's obedient servant
(or, Yours faithfully,)
JAMES GRIERSON.

No. 54.—Thanking a Patron

THE WARREN,
RUSTINGTON PEVEREL,
BERKSHIRE.
(*Date in full*).

MY LORD,

The Committee have the honour to acknowledge the receipt of your Lordship's letter of the 9th May and desire me to express their gratitude for the cheque which accompanied it and for your kindness in consenting to patronise our Fête and Sale of Work.

The Committee wish me to say how deeply they value your Lordship's interest and generosity and to express their sincere thanks for your valuable co-operation in our work.

I have the honour to be
Your Lordship's most obedient servant
JAMES GRIERSON.

No. 55.—Request to Serve on a Committee

HIGHFIELD COTTAGE,
PENWELL, BERKS.
(*Date in full*).

DEAR COLONEL HENDERSON,

I know you have very many calls upon your time but I am wondering whether you would kindly undertake yet one more activity, and agree to join the committee of the Penwell Bird Watching and Field Studies Association.

The Vicar has mentioned to me your own work in this connexion, during your years abroad, and such experience as yours would be invaluable in helping to develop our own local studies, which have begun in a small way but promise to become exceedingly interesting and useful.

Should you feel willing to undertake this, I will arrange for your name to be brought forward at the next meeting.

Yours sincerely,
IAN OWEN-JONES.

No. 56.—Asking for Votes for a Candidate for Admission to a Home

GALE HOUSE,
MORTLOCK.

(*Date in full*).

DEAR MR. HALFORD,

May I solicit your interest, and your vote, on behalf of Simon Perkins, whose admission into the South Eastern Home for Incurables I am anxious to secure? His is a most deserving case; I have known of him for some time. May I count upon your assistance for him, provided of course you have not already promised your support elsewhere? Should you wish, I can send you full particulars of the case, but for the present content myself with this brief appeal, since the election is still some time off. I know that the weight of your name would help considerably to turn the scale in this poor man's favour.

I remain
Yours sincerely,
ANTHONY HARGREAVES.

No. 57.—Requesting a Friend to be Best Man

"HIGHFIELDS,"
SANDERSTEAD.

(*Date in full*).

MY DEAR JACK,

Margaret has fixed the 18th of June for our wedding day and I am writing to ask you to do me the honour of being best man. It will mean a great deal to me if you will do me this great service, so I hope you will not let anything stand in the way. The wedding will take place in Margaret's parish, in London, and I hope you will be free to stay with me for a few days beforehand.

Yours,
HENRY BERRIDGE.

No. 58.—Requesting a Friend to Accept a Trusteeship

THE YEWS,
BOXMOOR.

(*Date in full*).

DEAR HERBERT,

I am in the process of making my Will, and wonder whether you would be so kind as to allow me to appoint you as an executor and also a Trustee in connexion with the arrangements I am making for the children.

Without wishing to belittle the service you will be doing me if you agree to this, I may say that the duties should not be too onerous. Your co-trustee would be Mr. Simon Stephens, an old friend of mine and a solicitor of the highest integrity, and in the event of the necessity arising, you could call freely upon his expert advice.

I ask this favour of you principally because of our long friendship, which assures me of your kindly interest in the beneficiaries of my will, and also because of the fact that you are some years younger than I. If you feel able to accept these duties, you will confer a great favour upon me, which, I need hardly say, will enable me to feel entirely happy about the future of the children.

Yours sincerely,
FRANK CARTER.

ENGAGEMENT AND MARRIAGE

No. 59.—A Proposal of Marriage

99 Lancaster Court,
W.2.

(*Date in full*).

Dearest Eleanor,

What I have to say in this letter may come as a surprise to you. Perhaps, though it may not. Such a sweet person as yourself must have had some inkling, before I came away, of the way my feelings were working. Indeed, it seemed to me that you held out hope and encouragement.

Since we have been separated, my dear, it has been absolutely crystal clear to me that you are the one woman in the world for me. To go through life at your side, to have the right to look after you, this seems to me to offer the only happiness that life holds. Can I hope that you feel the same? Will you agree to be my wife?

I would not trust this important question to a mere letter, believe me, if I saw any chance of putting it to you in person in the near future. But it looks as though this separation will last some little while yet, and I feel I cannot endure the uncertainty any longer. If you are able to say yes, darling, then I can work and wait patiently until we can be together again.

To be practical for a moment: as you know, I am dependent upon my own earnings, and these are not large at the present; but my firm is a good one and there is plenty of scope for me to rise. By the time I come home, I shall be in a position to marry; we shouldn't be rich, at first, but we could, I think, manage reasonably well.

Write to me as soon as you can.

Your loving,
Philip.

No. 60.—Acknowledging a Favourable Reply to a Proposal of Marriage

99 LANCASTER COURT,
W.2.

(*Date in full*).

MY DARLING ELEANOR,

Your letter today has made me the happiest man in the world. I wanted to dash out into the street and shout at the top of my voice, to let everyone know that the most glorious, beautiful, enchanting, clever, sweet girl in the world, has promised to be my wife. I walked to work and it was like walking on air. It wasn't till I noticed other people glancing curiously at me that I realised I had a beaming smile on my face despite the cold wind and a downpour that made everyone else look gloomy. So you see your power even extends to mitigating the elements!

I'll write again soon. Just now I'm almost too happy to think straight. How different the future looks, from what it did this time yesterday!

Always your own,
PHILIP.

No. 61.—From a Rejected Suitor

99 LANCASTER COURT,
W.2.

(*Date in full*).

DEAREST ELEANOR,

Your letter came yesterday and I must admit I felt pretty stunned by it. I suppose I should not have dared to hope, and yet I did. It had seemed to me that you were growing as fond of me as I was of you; but evidently my judgement of you was mistaken.

Things look pretty black to me just now, as you can perhaps understand. No doubt I shall eventually come to accept your decision in my heart, as my mind must already accept it. They say one gets over everything in time. But it is not going to be easy.

Believe me, my dear, when I say that although our lives will henceforth be along different paths, I shall always wish you well.

Always your sincere friend,
PHILIP.

No. 62.—From a Son, Announcing his Engagement

107 LANCASTER COURT,
W.2.

(*Date in full*).

MY DEAR MOTHER AND FATHER,

When I left home to come here, I imagine we all knew that big changes might take place before we met again and now I have some news which I hope will please you and make you happy.

I must have mentioned Julia Fane in previous letters, and probably you have guessed that we were becoming especially fond of one another. Now Julia has promised to marry me. I can't begin to tell you how happy I am, and how full of promise and purpose life now seems. She is a dear girl. I only wish I could bring her to see you both, for I know you would love her as much as I do.

We hope to be married in the spring, when I have taken my final qualifying exam; Julia wants to keep on with her job for a while after we are married—until we have got a home together, at any rate. We have been friends long enough to know our own minds, so there seems no reason to wait. But if there were any chance of your coming over for the wedding, we would like to fix the date to fit in with whatever you could arrange. Julia agrees with me that to have you with us on the great day is just the one thing needed to make our happiness complete. Her own parents, by the way, live just outside London; they have been most kind to me and seem to approve of our plans.

I will write again soon, and send a photo of Julia. hope to hear from you that you are pleased at my news.

Your loving son,
PHILIP.

No. 63.—Letter to a Son or Daughter who has written Announcing an Engagement

FIRTREE COTTAGE,
TRURO.

(*Date in full*).

MY DEAR CHILD,

Your letter announcing your forthcoming marriage made me feel very old and rather sentimental. However wise and sensible we parents may be (and I hope I am fairly sensible!) I suppose we always tend to think of our children as, well, children still, even when they are grown up. Now you are living your own life, making your own decisions and shouldering your own responsibilities. Well, my dear child, I have confidence in your judgement and feel sure you will have chosen wisely and well. You have too much sense to expect that life always goes smoothly; but to have the right partner at one's side is half the battle. It makes bad times less troublesome and good ones twice as good. I only wish your mother could have lived to share your happiness as I do. Please give my love to your sweetheart and say I hope we shall meet very soon.

Always your loving
FATHER.

No. 64.—From a Father asking a Gentleman to Cease his Attentions to his Daughter

THE TOWERS,
LANCASTER.

(*Date in full*).

DEAR SIR,

I have seen your letter of the 12th addressed to my daughter and I must ask you to refrain from writing to her, or attempting to see her, in future. My daughter is still very young and inexperienced and her mother and I prefer that for the time being she draws her friends only from among people we know well.

I trust that you will see that it is better for both of you that you should accept this letter as final, and comply with my request, as I have no wish to take steps that will be highly distasteful to me, and perhaps prejudicial to your own future.

I may add that I have spoken to my daughter about this matter and she understands that I do not wish this association to continue, and is prepared to respect my wishes in the matter. I trust you will do the same.

Yours faithfully,
JOHN PACKARD.

No. 65.—Congratulating a Friend upon His Engagement

99 KING'S ROAD,
N.10.

(*Date in full*).

MY DEAR HAROLD,

I am delighted to hear of your engagement and hasten to send you my warm congratulations. I can only say that I hope you will both be as happy in your married life as my wife and I have been.

Helen and I would be delighted if you will bring your fiancée to luncheon and introduce her to us at the earliest possible moment. We want to wish you both happiness in person.

Yours always,
WALTER LOWE.

No. 66.—To a Young Man, Remonstrating upon His Engagement

CARLTON VILLA,
TEDDINGTON.

(*Date in full*).

MY DEAR CHRISTOPHER,

I was very surprised to read in the paper this morning of your engagement and could have wished that I had learned of it first from yourself and not through the press. I trust, my dear boy, that you know what you are about. Marriage is really a serious undertaking, even nowadays when so many young people seem to embark upon it very lightly. I know nothing of your fiancée personally, but I do feel you are very young, with your career still to make, and ought to hesitate before you embark upon the responsibilities of marriage. I trust that your fiancée is the kind of girl who will be a real help to you, put your career first, and share your burdens in the difficult times that may lie ahead.

I remain,
Your affectionate uncle,
ROBERT TURNER.

No. 67.—From a Gentleman to his Fiancée

Duke of York Mansions,
Battersea, S.W.11.
(*Date in full*).

Dearest Irene,

Your sweet letter came this morning—I wish you could have seen how eagerly I tore it open and how many times I have read and re-read it during the day. I can hardly believe that all these sweet things you say are really meant for me.

Do you find it hard to be patient till that day comes? I do, terribly. Life seems to be standing still, until we can start the great adventure of building up a life together. The flat I have here is pleasant enough—I have told you before about the charming view from my balcony but it needs you here to make it really a home. My work in the city is interesting and rewarding, but I need you to work for to give it a real meaning.

Last evening I went to visit the Browns, to whom I had been given a letter of introduction. They were charming people who made me very welcome. It made me long for the day when we have our own home, and can entertain our friends; how proud of you I shall be! Mrs. Brown asked me all about you, and it was such a delight to be able to talk about you, to such sympathetic listeners.

Things are going well at the office. Coming here has meant a temporary separation from you but will, I think, bring nearer the day when we are in a position to marry. So you see, things are not standing still, and though the waiting may be tedious, it is all going to be worth while in the end.

Write again soon, darling, even if you haven't much news. Just to see your writing brightens the day more than I can tell you.

Your loving
Jack.

No. 68.—Inquiring why a Lady has not Written

DUKE OF YORK MANSIONS,
BATTERSEA, S.W.11.
(*Date in full*).

DEAREST IRENE,

It is nearly three weeks since you wrote and I am so worried in case something is wrong. I tell myself that it can't be that you are ill, or have met with an accident, because surely someone would have let me know. Still, I can't help worrying and imaging the worst. And even if all is well with you, I still feel cause to worry and wonder what is the reason for this long silence. Do write soon and tell me if anything is wrong, for I shall not rest till I hear from you.

Yours always,
JACK.

No. 69.—Upon the Breaking of an Engagement

MOSSDALE,
BICKLEY.
(*Date in full*).

DEAR PHILIP,

I have just seen the announcement in the paper of the breaking off of your engagement. This kind of thing is bound to be pretty painful and embarrassing and there isn't much that one can say to help matters. Believe me, all your friends are with you in spirit at this time. If it would help to drop in for a chat any time, we are in most evenings.

Yours,
RAYMOND.

BUSINESS

No. 70.—Stopping Payment of a Cheque

THE DELL,
BROMLEY, KENT.
(*Date in full*).

The Manager,
West Kent Bank Ltd.,
Tonbridge.

DEAR SIR,
Please stop payment of my cheque No. 1000 for £73 15s. 0d. dated the 16th instant, drawn in favour of Arthur Brown Ltd. and signed by myself.

Yours faithfully,
JAMES HANKINSON.

No. 71.—Opening a new Bank Account

BEECHMOUNT LODGE,
SEVENOAKS.
(*Date in full*).

The Manager,
West Kent Bank Ltd.,
Tonbridge.

DEAR SIR,
I enclose cheque value £200 (two hundred pounds)

Please place this to the credit of a new account to be opened under the name of "Jonathan Morley, 'B' Account." I trust you will be good enough to honour all cheques presented to you to the debit of the above account.

Yours faithfully,
JONATHAN MORLEY.

No. 72.—Engaging a Solicitor

23 STATION ROAD,
BIRKENHEAD.
(*Date in full*).

DEAR SIR,

Your name has been given to me by Mr. James Henderson for whom I understand you act in legal matters. I need the help of a solicitor experienced in house purchase matters, and would be obliged if you would act for me in this and other concerns from now onwards. I look forward to hearing that you are able to do this.

Yours faithfully,
STEPHEN LAURISTON.

No. 73.—Changing a Solicitor

23 STATION ROAD,
BIRKENHEAD.
(*Date in full*).

DEAR SIR,

As you know, I am the sole executor of the will drawn up by you for my late aunt, Mrs. Sarah Daw. It would simplify matters considerably and make things easier for me if this matter of my aunt's will were handled from now on by my own solicitors, Messrs. Mann, Chandler and Nephew. Will you kindly forward them the relevant papers? If you will let me have your account for the work already done in the matter, I will attend to it at once.

Yours faithfully,
STEPHEN LAURISTON.

No. 74.—Changing a Doctor, National Health Service

20 CROSBY GARDENS,
NORTH FINCHLEY.
(*Date in full*).

DEAR DR. GROVE,

For some while I have not felt happy about my family's being on your list. Peter's cough, for example, has not improved as I feel it should. I realise you are extremely busy and perhaps it would be better if we registered with another medical man who has more time for these obstinate cases. Will you kindly accept this notification of our withdrawal from your list.

Yours faithfully,
JOHN EVANS.

No. 75.—To a New Doctor, National Health Service

20 CROSBY GARDENS,
NORTH FINCHLEY.
(*Date in full*).

DEAR DR. PARRY,

Would you kindly accept myself and my family as patients on your list under the National Health Service? We were formerly patients of Dr. Grove, but I have felt it wise for various reasons to make a change. I enclose our N.H.S. cards.

Yours faithfully,
JOHN EVANS.

No. 76.—Changing Doctors, Private

OAKLANDS,
GROVE ROAD,
CROYDON.

(*Date in full*).

DEAR DR. MILTON,

For some time I have not felt satisfied with the progress of my wife's illness, and rather than let things drag on in this way any longer, I think it might be wise to try a change of treatment. Thank you for all you have done for my wife. It you will kindly send your account, I will attend to it at once.

Yours faithfully,
IAN NICHOLLS.

No. 77.—To a New Doctor, Private

OAKLANDS,
GROVE ROAD,
CROYDON.

(*Date in full*).

DEAR DR. PARRY,

Would you kindly call at this address as soon as possible? My wife has been ill with a stomach complaint for some time for which she has been attended by Dr. Milton. As things have not improved, I feel it wise to try a change of treatment and have notified Dr. Milton accordingly. I should be glad if you would take charge of the case from now on.

Yours truly,
IAN NICHOLLS.

No. 78.—A Boy's Application for Employment

HIGH ROAD,
WOOD GREEN, N.22.
(*Date in full*).

DEAR SIR,

I beg to apply for the vacant situation in your office. Having only recently left school I have no previous experience of an office boy's duties, but I am good at arithmetic, able to write neatly and clearly, and have been taught to be careful, punctual, and reliable.

My father, who has a hardware store in Wood Green, will be glad to bring me for an interview should you think my application worthy of consideration. My age is fifteen. I enclose a copy of a testimonial from my former headmaster.

I am
Your obedient servant,
FRANCIS WALTON.

No. 79.—Application for Position as Book-Keeper

777 JOHN STREET,
MANCHESTER.
(*Date in full*).

DEAR SIRS,

In reply to your advertisement in this morning's *Guardian* I beg to apply for the position. I have a thorough knowledge of book-keeping and accounts, having been for the past seven years in the accounts department of Messrs. Hancock and Truman, who would, I feel sure, give you an assurance of my personal character and abilities. My reason for wishing to leave my present firm is, that I feel a larger office would offer more scope for the promotion which, with my experience and at my age (I am 27) I should now be looking for.

I shall be glad to call upon you by appointment for a personal interview if you wish.

Yours faithfully,
JAMES MARPLE.

No. 80.—Application for a Technical Post

28 COLLEGE STREET,
HARROW.

(*Date in full*).

DEAR SIR,

Further to your advertisement in this morning's *Observer* I should be glad if you would consider my application for the vacancy. I am 24 years of age and have my Ordinary National Certificate in Electrical Engineering. I have been two years with the firm of Edgware Electronics Ltd., whose name is doubtless known to you and who would furnish a reference if required; with them I have acquired a very good technical background in resistance welding and have also had experience of dealing with customers both in person and by correspondence. In applying for the position you advertise I am, frankly, seeking to improve my financial prospects, but apart from this, I hope to achieve a position of more scope, such as is offered by a firm with so wide a range of interests as yours.

I look forward to hearing from you in due course.

Yours faithfully,
ERNEST JOHNSON.

No. 81.—Application for Position in a Laboratory

19 Seldon Avenue,
London, N.10.
(*Date in full*).

Dear Sirs,

In reply to your advertisement in this morning's *Times* for a supervisor of your analytical laboratory, I beg to apply for the position.

I am a B.Sc. of London University, having specialised in chemistry; since coming down I have been working as assistant to the director of the food Laboratory of the Universal Canning Company. My age is 28.

I can call upon you by appointment if you wish; a Friday is usually my best day, but I can arrange to come at some other time if that would be more convenient.

Yours faithfully,
William Lowe.

No. 82.—From a Clerk to a Firm asking if they can place him

The Dell,
Bromley, Kent.
(*Date in full*).

Dear Sirs,

Knowing how rapidly your Insurance business is growing, it has occurred to me to ask whether you are wanting another assistant with insurance experience. For ten years I have been with Mr. George Marlowe getting the all-round knowledge that experience in a small firm gives, but now I have got as far there as I can go. I am studying for my professional examinations. My salary for the past two years has been £750 and I should not make a change for less. My relations with Mr. Marlowe have been entirely pleasant and I know he would answer any questions you may wish to put to him regarding my character and ability.

Yours faithfully,
WILLIAM BLISS.

No. 83.—Asking for a Letter of Recommendation

THE DELL,
BROMLEY, KENT.
(*Date in full*).

DEAR MR. MARLOWE,

My application to Messrs. Illingworth Bros. has proved successful beyond expectation. They offer me a position in their Fire Insurance department and a worth-while salary, but they want a written letter of recommendation from yourself and information as to how soon you can spare me.

Apologising for intruding upon your holiday and thanking you for many past kindnesses and (in anticipation) for this fresh favour.

I remain,
Yours truly,
WILLIAM BLISS.

No. 84.—Letter of Recommendation

HOTEL METROPOLE,
TORQUAY.
(*Date in full*).

DEAR SIRS,

Mr. William Bliss has been with me ten years and has learned all about the business that I can teach anyone. He has a sound understanding of insurance business and is of unimpeachable integrity. With the opportunities afforded by a large business such as yours he should go far. I part with him with great reluctance.

Yours truly,
G. MARLOWE.

No. 85.—From a Young Man who has been Recommended to a Merchant

12 ESSEX ROAD,
LONDON, S.W.11.
(*Date in full*).

DEAR SIR,

Mr. Watkins having promised to do his best to interest you on my behalf, I am now venturing to write to you myself. The leather business has always attracted me and I know that in this industry the name of Plowden and Pink stands alone. Mr. Watkins says that you will be willing to see me next Tuesday before ten. Unless I hear to the contrary I shall call upon you at nine-thirty on that date.

Yours faithfully,
PAUL WINDERMERE.

No. 86.—Inquiry into the Character of a Prospective Employee

HORSE AND HOUNDS HOTEL,
NEWBURY.
(*Date in full*).

DEAR SIR,

Mr. Colin Cross, whom I am thinking of engaging as a clerk and book-keeper at this hotel, has referred me to you for his character. Would you mind, therefore, telling me what you know as to his ability and trustworthiness?

Yours faithfully,
T. BROWNING.

No. 87.—Reply to above

KITTLE AND KEMPTON LTD.,
92 THE MALL,
BEDFORD.

(*Date in full*).

DEAR SIR,

Mr. Cross was in our counting house for eighteen months and we were quite satisfied with him. He had then a fair knowledge of book-keeping, which he may have added to in the six months since he left us. In general knowledge and intelligence he is above the average.

Yours faithfully,
T. J. KITTLE.

No. 88.—A Chauffeur Seeking Employment

200 JOHN STREET,
S.W.9.

(*Date in full*).

DEAR SIR,

I beg to apply for the post of chauffeur as advertised in *The Times* of today.

For five years I was a taxi-driver in London, so have a thorough knowledge of the roads in the metropolis. I also spent two years as mechanic in the Woking Motor Works, where I gained a through and practical knowledge of the mechanism of a car.

I have a clean driving licence and am a teetotaller.

For the last three years I have been in the employ of A. Bradley, Esq., of the Manor House, Streatham. This gentleman is leaving England to settle in Kenya, this being my only reason for leaving his service. He has kindly agreed to act as a reference.

I trust, Sir, that you will grant me an interview, when

I may clearly put my qualifications before you and answer any questions you may wish to put to me.

Yours respectfully,
JOHN CARTER.

No. 89.—To Business Acquaintances from One Setting up in Business on his own Account

33 MOOR ROAD,
TONBRIDGE.
(*Date in full*).

DEAR SIRS,

I beg to inform you that after twenty years' service with Messrs. Spriggs, I am leaving them in order to commence business on my own account at the above address. I have conducted many transactions with yourselves and I trust you will accord me your good-will and consideration in my new venture. Any instructions from you will, of course, be given the most prompt attention.

Yours faithfully,
JOHN ALLEN.

No. 90—From an Employee, Giving Notice

207 MANOR HOUSE ROAD,
WIMBLEDON.
(*Date in full*).

DEAR SIR,

I beg herewith to tender my resignation of my appointment in your office. I much regret leaving a place where I have received many kindnesses and made a number of friends, but I feel I must seek an appointment with a larger salary and opportunities for more rapid promotion than I can expect at present. Please, therefore, accept my notice to leave on the 31st of next month.

Yours faithfully,
HENRY JONES.

No. 91.—From an Employee, asking for an Increase in Salary

26 OREGON ROAD,
STAINES.

(*Date in full*).

DEAR MR. WRIGHTSON,

May I raise with you the matter of my salary, which has stood now for nearly two years at the same figure, £——. Since then, the work of this department has increased very considerably, and, as you know, I now have to supervise the work of four juniors instead of the original two. I think it is fair to say, too, that the department is making a big contribution to the success of the firm as a whole. This being so, I feel that my increased usefulness to the firm justifies me in asking for a substantial rise, and I hope you will agree to this.

Yours faithfully,
WALTER FORD.

No. 92.—An Unfavourable Reply

MORLEY WRIGHTSON LTD.,
26 OREGON ROAD,
STAINES.

(*Date in full*).

DEAR MR. FORD,

Thank you for raising the matter of your salary. I regret, however, that we cannot give you any rise immediately. Business at present doesn't warrant it, but the outlook is improving and we have plans for extending the scope of our business in the near future. When this happens, I shall hope to be able to reconsider your salary, more favourably.

Yours truly,
HAROLD WRIGHTSON.

No. 93.—Favourable Reply

MORLEY, WRIGHTSON LTD.,
26 OREGON ROAD,
STAINES.

(*Date in full*).

DEAR MR. FORD,

Thank you for raising the matter of your salary. Although the figure you mention is rather more than is usual in the trade for the responsibilities you at present carry, I am acceding to your request because before very long there will be work for you more onerous and responsible. I am notifying the firm's cashier to this effect, as from this week.

Yours truly,
HAROLD WRIGHTSON.

No. 94.—An Employee Acknowledging an Increase in Salary

26 OREGON ROAD,
STAINES.

(*Date in full*).

DEAR MR. WRIGHTSON,

Thank you indeed for the very substantial addition to my salary. I trust my increased usefulness to the firm will amply justify it.

Yours faithfully,
WALTER FORD.

No. 95.—Letter Explaining Absence from Business

24 Wick Lane,
Kilburn, N.W.6.
(*Date in full*).

Dear Sirs,

Confirming my telephone message this morning, I regret to inform you that I am suffering from an attack of influenza and have been ordered to bed for a few days. I enclose a certificate from my doctor and trust that my absence will cause no serious inconvenience.

Yours sincerely,
William Jones.

No. 96.—Another, ditto

Galton Villas,
East Dulwich, S.E.22.
(*Date in full*).

Dear Mr. Spencer,

In explanation of my telephone message to the office this morning, I write to say that my wife, who has been ill for some time, was taken worse last night and her condition is causing the gravest anxiety. I shall return to the office as soon as the immediate danger has passed. I trust my absence is not causing too much inconvenience.

Yours sincerely,
William Jones.

No. 97.—Letter of Credit

17 Somerset Road,
Leeds.
(*Date in full*).

Dear Sirs,

This letter will be delivered to you by Mr. John Marshall, eldest son of Mr. Marshall, the chairman of our firm, who will visit your city preparatory to a tour through India. His drafts (the amount £500) you will oblige us by honouring and placing to our debit at the current rate of exchange. Any personal attention you may be able to show Mr. John Marshall will confer an additional obligation on

Yours faithfully,
MARTON & CO.

No. 98.—From a Tradesman, Soliciting Custom

23 HIGH STREET,
DITTON-ON-CANE.
(*Date in full*).

DEAR SIR,

I understand you have taken "The Birches" which is not very far from my shop. I venture to ask for your esteemed patronage. I can supply you with provisions of the highest quality which, as you will see from the enclosed list, compare favourably with those of the largest stores, including deep-freeze products of all kinds.

Trusting to be favoured with your orders, which shall receive my best attention,

I remain,
Your obedient servant,
JOHN TAYLOR.

No. 99.—A Tradesman Commencing Business

42 HIGH STREET,
MACKLIN.
(*Date in full*).

DEAR SIR,

I beg to inform you that I have commenced business this day at the above address as a draper and haberdasher, and if favoured with your orders, shall be greatly indebted.

My stock has been selected with great care from the leading wholesalers in London and elsewhere and I have made arrangements to add from time to time the newest lines as they are produced by the manufacturers. My own experience as a buyer with Messrs. Harridges enables me to purchase the most approved goods as cheaply as any of the long-established drapers in the town, and the assistants I have engaged are qualified in every respect to give satisfaction.

I enclose a price list of the principal articles in stock.

I am,
Your obedient Servant,
ROBERT PHILLIPS.

No. 100.—Addressing a Wholesale Firm on the Same Subject

42 HIGH STREET,
MACKLIN.

(*Date in full*).

DEAR SIRS,

I beg to inform you that I have arranged to carry on business as a haberdasher at the above address and shall require from time to time to make additions to my stock. I am prepared to pay cash for the first few purchases and, as the accounts in this neighbourhood are quarterly, meet further engagements by bill at three months' date.

Having every confidence in your firm I shall be glad to give you my preference if I am placed upon the same footing as your other customers, both as regards money matters and the carrying-out of orders. With a view to opening up correspondence, may I refer you to Messrs. Brown of Luton, who will give you every satisfaction as regards my financial position.

Yours faithfully,
ROBERT PHILLIPS.

No. 101.—Transmitting Order for Goods

42 HIGH STREET,
MACKLIN.

(*Date in full*).

DEAR SIRS,

I am obliged by your prompt reply to my previous letter and now beg to place in your hands an order for certain additions to my stock. As these goods are wanted almost daily, I shall be glad to receive them as early as possible. I need hardly remind you that much of my future business depends upon the quality of the articles I stock at present, and I feel assured your goods will afford my customers no grounds for complaint.

Please find enclosed order sheet.

Yours faithfully,
ROBERT PHILLIPS.

No. 102.—Letter Respecting Damaged Goods

42 HIGH STREET,
MACKLIN.

(*Date in full*).

DEAR SIRS,

I regret to inform you that four of the linen tablecloths delivered here in execution of my order dated 14th inst. are unsaleable; they are torn in several places. I have repacked them and delivered the parcel to your carriers with instructions to return it to you.

Please either substitute perfect pieces for the rejects or credit me with £8, the invoice cost of the latter.

Yours faithfully,
ROBERT PHILLIPS.

No. 103.—Answer to the Above

999 CANNON STREET,
LONDON, E.C.4.
(*Date in full*).

DEAR SIR,

The contents of your letter of yesterday's date surprised us considerably as our warehousemen have explicit instructions to supply our customers with perfect goods only, and return the unsound, to the manufacturer. It is clear, however, that your goods must have been packed without examination. We regret exceedingly that you have been put to the trouble of returning the rejects and we are forwarding to your address 4 perfect tablecloths to replace the others.

Yours faithfully,
MOORE, ROBINSON & CO. LTD.

No. 104.—From a Shopkeeper to a Merchant

26 QUEEN'S PARADE,
MAIDSTONE.
(*Date in full*).

DEAR SIR,

Would you be good enough to let me know by return the current prices of the articles named on the enclosed list. If I find that they allow a reasonable profit, I should like to order in quantity.

Yours faithfully,
HENRY CROSS.

No. 105.—Reply to Above

45 RIVER STREET,
OXFORD.
(*Date in full*).

DEAR SIR,

In reply to your request of yesterday's date, I enclose our most recent price list, showing both wholesale and retail prices, with purchase tax at current rates where applicable.

Yours faithfully,
GEORGE HYDE.

No. 106.—Tradesman's Letter sending Quarterly Account

1000 RYE LANE,
LONDON, S.E.15.
(*Date in full*).

SIR,

The March quarter having expired, I beg to enclose statement of your account, amounting to £12 8s. 4d. I trust the articles gave satisfaction.

I remain,
Your obedient servant,
FREDERICK HARRIS.

No. 107.—Customer Complaining about Goods

THE GROVE,
PECKHAM, S.E.15.
(*Date in full*).

DEAR SIR,

I return your bill for the March quarter for correction as the articles supplied have, I am sorry to say, proved far from satisfactory. The two rugs have, unfortunately, faded considerably even in the short time they have been in use, and the blue one is also showing signs of wear already. If you care to send a representative, I shall be happy to let him inspect them, and beg to state that I consider your account should be reduced by at least 25 per cent., to compensate for the faults in the quality of the goods.

Yours faithfully,
JAMES WILKINSON.

No. 108.—Another, ditto

26 QUEEN'S PARADE,
MAIDSTONE.
(*Date in full*).

DEAR SIR,

I return your bill for correction as the prices charged therein are in excess of those of any other tradesmen in the neighbourhood. The articles supplied, also, were of an inferior quality and not what we expected from a firm of your standing. I consider the overcharges altogether amount to fully 25 per cent., and ask you to reduce your account accordingly.

Yours faithfully,
HENRY CROSS.

No. 109.—Reply of Tradesman

1000 RYE LANE,
LONDON, S.E.15.
(*Date in full*).

SIR,

Although I consider my bill entirely free from anything in the shape of an overcharge, I am willing, on this occasion, to allow you twenty per cent discount for cash. I must point out that I cannot on any future occasion make a similar allowance, otherwise your account would obviously become a source of loss to me. I look forward to receiving your cheque by return of post.

Yours faithfully,
FREDERICK HARRIS.

No. 110.—Reply, Negatively

1000 RYE LANE,
LONDON, S.E.15.
(*Date in full*).

DEAR SIR,

In reply to your letter, I must point out that my charges, so far from being excessive, are quite as moderate as those of any firm in the business, and so slightly above cost that should I make a deduction as you suggest, I should be a great loser. I must also point out that yours is the first complaint I have received as regards the quality of goods I supply. It would have been more satisfactory to all concerned had you mentioned before this that you considered you were being served with inferior goods; since your orders were given throughout the quarter without complaint, there was every reason to believe you were satisfied. I must therefore request you to pay the amount of the bill in full.

Yours faithfully,
FREDERICK HARRIS.

No. 111.—Letter asking for Payment of Account

1000 RYE LANE,
LONDON, S.E.15.
(*Date in full*).

DEAR SIR,

Owing to my own present committments I am obliged

to ask you kindly to settle my bill for the March quarter by return of post. Were I in a position to wait longer for settlement I should have been happy to do so, but it is not possible. I beg, therefore, that you will send a cheque without further delay. The amount of the bill rendered is £12 8s. 4d.

Yours faithfully,
FREDERICK HARRIS.

No. 112.—Letter Demanding Payment

1000 RYE LANE,
LONDON, S.E.15.
(*Date in full*).

DEAR SIR,

Having applied to you repeatedly but ineffectively for a settlement of my bill—the amount being £12 8s. 4d.—I have now regretfully to inform you that unless it is paid before 12 o'clock noon tomorrow I shall place the matter in the hands of my solicitor.

Yours faithfully,
FREDERICK HARRIS.

No. 113.—Letter Promising to Pay

THE GROVE,
PECKHAM, S.E.15.
(*Date in full*).

DEAR SIR,

I am sorry that your bill has remained unpaid so long. This has been entirely owing to my inability to collect my own outstanding debts which amount to a considerable sum. I have now, however, a promise of payment on the

14th instant, and trust to be able to settle your own bill on that date.

Yours faithfully,
JAMES WILKINSON.

No. 114.—Another, ditto

99 CHURCH STREET,
GLOUCESTER.
(*Date in full*).

DEAR SIR,

Having a bill for a large amount to meet besides your own, I beg your indulgence for a few days, say till the 10th inst., at the expiry of which I hope to be able to remit the sum in full.

Yours faithfully,
JOSEPH KING.

No. 115.—To a Tradesman, Repudiating Liability for Debts Incurred by a Wife

CRANSTON SQUARE, W.1.
(*Date in full*).

GENTLEMEN,

I beg to draw your attention to the notice I have today published in *The Times* of today's date, repudiating liability for all debts contracted by my wife (Caroline Elizabeth Sophia Jones) and announcing that she has no authority to pledge my credit. Please understand that from now onwards I can only be responsible for orders signed by myself personally.

Yours faithfully,
JOHN JONES.

No. 116.—From a Debtor, Asking for Time to Pay

50 Nero Road,
Wimbledon, S.W.19.
(*Date in full*).

Dear Sir,

I regret to inform you that business has lately been very bad and consequently I find myself unable to settle your account just at present. I hope you will kindly accord me a longer term of credit and accept my assurance that I will do all in my power to remit the amount in full as soon as possible.

Yours faithfully,
Charles Furman.

No. 117.—To a Creditor, Announcing the Filing of a Petition in Bankruptcy

29 Princess Margaret Road,
Millstones.
(*Date in full*).

Dear Sir,

I regret to inform you that I have been compelled to file my petition in bankruptcy. This was necessary in the interests of my creditors, for Messrs. Skinflint and Scrooge were pressing me unduly. My failure was due to the difficulty in collecting accounts and consequent lack of ready capital but I am hopeful that the estate will realise twenty shillings in the pound.

Thanking you for your many favours,

Yours faithfully,
Alfred Mannesty.

INQUIRIES AND REFERENCES

No. 118.—Inquiry as to Responsibility

77 CHOURINGEE,
CALCUTTA.

(*Date in full*).

DEAR SIRS,

We are thinking of appointing Messrs. Lyon Crocker & Co. of Billiter Street, as our London Agents, and shall be obliged if you will tell us whether you have found them satisfactory in that capacity.

Yours faithfully,
BROWN & STEVENSON LTD.

No. 119.—Requesting a Reference

BOW LANE,
LONDON, E.C.4.

(*Date in full*).

DEAR SIR,

We are obliged to you for the order placed with our representative, Mr. Stock, and shall be pleased to fill it upon the terms mentioned, if you will kindly furnish us with a London reference. We make it an invariable rule not to open credit accounts without this formality.

Yours faithfully,
WREN & HISLOP, LTD.

No. 120.—Reply to Above

THE ARCADE,
STOURVILLE-ON-SEA.
(*Date in full*).

Messrs. Wren & Hislop.

DEAR SIRS,

You can apply to Messrs. Macgregor & Co. Ltd. of Wood Street, or to the Tower Co. of Houndsditch, with both of whom I have dealt with for several years. Your Mr. Stock knows of my standing in Stourville.

Yours faithfully,
JOHN MALLOCK.

No. 121.—Application for a Reference

BOW LANE,
LONDON, E.C.4.
(*Date in full*).

The Tower Co.,
Houndsditch.

DEAR SIRS,

Mr. J. Mallock of Stourville-on-Sea has referred us to you. Can you please say if you consider him worthy of credit, up to the sum of, say, £50. We should be obliged for your opinion, in confidence of course.

Yours faithfully,
WREN & HISLOP.

No. 122.—Reply to above

HOUNDSDITCH, E.1.
(*Date in full*).

DEAR SIRS,

In reply to your inquiry about Mr. J. Mallock of Stourville-on-Sea, we should not hesitate to give him credit up to the sum you mention—or considerably more, for that matter. Our dealings with him have always been most satisfactory.

Yours faithfully,
THE TOWER CO. LTD.

No. 123.—Another, negative

HOUNDSDITCH, E.1.
(*Date in full*).

DEAR SIRS,

In reply to your inquiry about Mr. J. Mallock of Stourville, we regret our inability to give you any information that would be helpful to you. Our own dealings with Mr. Mallock have not been extensive enough for us to be able to speak with confidence about him, in a matter of this kind.

Yours faithfully,
THE TOWER CO. LTD.

No. 124.—Asking for a Business Introduction

19 SELDON AVENUE,
LONDON, N.10.
(*Date in full*).

DEAR MRS. HENDERSON,

I wonder if you would be kind enough to give me an introduction to Mr. Leslie Appleby whom I believe you know. I want to see him upon a matter of business which I think may have certain advantages for him as well as for myself. I shall be greatly obliged to you if you can bring about a meeting between us.

Yours sincerely,
ALFRED PATERSON.

LANDLORD AND TENANT

No. 125.—From a Tenant, making a Complaint

42 CLYDE ROAD,
CANONBURY.
(*Date in full*).

DEAR SIR,

I shall be obliged if you will instruct your representative to call here at once to see to some pipes. In the recent frost, a water pipe burst; a plumber I sent for has repaired it to the best of his ability but tells me that the pipe is so thin that no reliance can be placed upon it and that it should be replaced without delay. I ask you to attend to the matter immediately, as neglect now may cause considerable damage to the property, expense to yourself and inconvenience to my family and myself.

Yours faithfully,
ARTHUR MORGAN.

No. 126.—From a Tenant, complaining of Damage

90 ST. ANN'S ROAD,
BATTERSEA.
(*Date in full*).

DEAR MR. SMITH,

I am sorry to report that the heavy rain of the last few days has found a weak spot in the roof of this house and that last night the ceiling in the larger back bedroom fell in, breaking some of the mirrors and spoiling a new carpet bought for the room. I have written to your agent about the necessary repairs to the roof and no doubt he will attend to this promptly.

I feel that I also have some claim upon you for the damage to my belongings. The carpet was bought only a few weeks ago from Messrs. Borage's (I can show you the receipt for it). I have asked them to call and estimate the cost of cleaning and repairing it, if this can be done; otherwise, a replacement may be necessary. Both the mirrors will have to be replaced. I should be glad to have your views on this matter.

Yours truly,
WILLIAM GOLDER.

No. 127.—Requesting Time to Pay Rent

99 ENFIELD GROVE,
HAMPSTEAD, N.W.3.
(*Date in full*).

DEAR SIR,

I have been your tenant some years now in this house and have never failed to pay my rent quarterly when duc. I am sorry to say, however, that in consequence of a variety of difficulties and setbacks, it is impossible for me to find the amount of the rent which falls due next week. I would appreciate it very much if you would allow the matter to stand over for a week or two, when I hope to be able to find the full amount owing, or at any rate to send something on account with the balance soon after.

Yours faithfully,
EDWARD STANFORD.

No. 128.—Reply to above

42 WINTERBOURNE STREET,
CHELSEA, S.W.3.
(*Date in full*).

DEAR MR. STANFORD,

In reply to your letter of yesterday, it will be quite in order for you to leave payment of your rent for a week or two, until your affairs improve. I am very sorry to hear of your difficulties and trust things will soon take a turn for the better.

Yours sincerely,
SIDNEY GREY.

No. 129.—Asking to be Relieved of a Lease

99 ENFIELD GROVE,
HAMPSTEAD, N.W.3.

DEAR SIR,

An unexpected change for the worse in my financial situation (caused by the expropriation of my shares in Ruritanian Oil Properties, following the revolution in that country three months ago) makes it imperative that I should remove to a less expensive house. Would you, therefore, kindly consider cancelling my lease of these premises and releasing me from my obligation to you. The premises are in good condition and the garden attractive and as the lease has several years to run I imagine you would easily find another tenant to take over the remainder of it. It would be a great relief to me to be released from the agreement for frankly, the house is far more expensive than I can afford now.

Yours faithfully,
EDWARD STANFORD.

No. 130.—Receipt for Rent

99 Craneborough Road,
Matcham.

(*Date in full*).

Received of Mrs. Margaret Doyle, the sum of £25, being one quarter's rent due on Lady Day last for the premises occupied by her at No. 300, Charles Street, Matcham.

Henry Jones-Smith.

No. 131.—To a House Agent Stating Requirements

The Hollies,
Meadow Lane,
Broxbourne.

(*Date in full*).

Dear Sirs,

I am anxious to rent a house, at not more than £400 a year, in the neighbourhood of Hendon. It should be in a quiet and cheerful road, with easy access to shops and transport, and be suitable for entertaining. I need four bedrooms. I do not want a repairing lease.

Will you let me know of any houses on your books which may be suitable?

Yours faithfully,
Charles Snow.

No. 132.—Inquiring about Hotel Accommodation

7 FRENCH STREET,
N.W.5.

(*Date in full*).

To the Manager,
The Ship Hotel,
Brightlingsea.

DEAR SIR,

Your hotel has been recommended to me by a friend, Mr. John Bowman. As I hope to visit Brightlingsea in June, will you let me have a note of your terms and also let me know whether you can let me have two double rooms facing the sea between June 12th and June 26th. One room would be for my wife and myself, the other for our boys aged 5 and 6.

Yours faithfully,
THOMAS WILTON.

No. 133.—Reserving Hotel Accommodation

7 FRENCH STREET,
N.W.5.

(*Date in full*).

DEAR SIR,

Thank you for sending me your prospectus and a note of your terms. These are satisfactory, so will you please reserve for us the rooms mentioned in your letter.

Yours faithfully,
THOMAS WILTON.

No. 134.—Booking a Steamer Passage

200 Hans Place,
S.W.3.

(*Date in full*).

Dear Sirs,

I wish to sail for New York in H.M.S. Majestia, arriving on or before June 10th. I shall require two 1st class passages. Would you kindly forward me particulars of the stateroom accommodation available and the relevant sailing dates? I prefer deck cabins.

Yours faithfully,
John Borden.

The General Navigation Co. Ltd.,
300 Cockspur Street, S.W.1.

No. 135.—Booking Seats in an Aeroplane

24 James Street,
Berkeley Square, W.1.
(*Date in full*).

Dear Sir,

Confirming our telephone conversation of this morning, kindly reserve me two seats in the plane leaving London Airport for Paris at 2 p.m. on Wednesday, June 12th. I shall also be glad if you will let me know the connexions between London and the Airport. I enclose cheque for the price of the seats.

Yours faithfully,
Anthony Brocklehurst.

No. 136.—Complaint to Local Authority

HURST MANOR,
INGLEWICK.

(*Date in full*).

To the Clerk of the Rural District Council,
Inglewick.

DEAR SIR,

As a resident and ratepayer I must complain about the persistent failure of the street lighting along Hurstwood Lane and Inglewick Road (the part that runs alongside the golf course.) Not only are these two roads in a bad state of repair so that good lighting is absolutely essential if one is to walk along them in comfort, but also, the absence of lights is a positive encouragement to loiterers and bad characters, so that womenfolk around here are nervous of walking along the roads after dark. Will you kindly take whatever steps are necessary to see that these lighting breakdowns do not happen again?

Yours faithfully,
HENRY MILLINGTON.

No. 137.—Letter to an Insurance Company

THE YEWS,
BOXMOOR.

(*Date in full*).

DEAR SIRS,

I have recently bought my wife a diamond ring and wish to insure it against loss, theft, damage, etc. The cost of the ring and the sum for which I wish to insure it is £500. Will you kindly send your representative to arrange terms, and in the meantime, I should be obliged if you can hold me covered as from the date of this letter.

Yours faithfully,
JOHN STRATTON.

No. 138.—To a Publisher submitting a Novel

THE LIMES,
HARTFIELD,
CANTERBURY.
(*Date in full*).

DEAR SIRS,

I am sending you under separate cover by registered post the typescript of a novel, "Love in Bloom" which I have just completed.

You will recall that you published my biography of Beethoven fifteen years ago—a work which was a success both critically and commercially—it achieved a sale of 30,000 copies.

I hope your opinion of this, my latest book, will be sufficiently favourable to encourage you to make an offer for its publication, but I enclose stamps for its return if your verdict proves adverse.

Yours faithfully,
THOMAS WILTON.

No. 139.—To a Publisher Requesting a Decision

THE LIMES,
HARTFIELD,
CANTERBURY.
(*Date in full*).

DEAR SIRS,

On the ——— of ——— I sent you by registered post the typescript of my novel "Love in Bloom", but I have so far heard nothing from you.

Assuming it reached you safely, I shall be obliged if you will return the manuscript to me, unless, as I hope may be the case, you have any proposal to make to me regarding it.

Yours faithfully,
THOMAS WILTON.

No. 140.—Claiming from an Insurance Company

THE YEWS,
KING'S ROAD,
BOXMOOR.

(*Date in full*).

DEAR SIRS,

In accordance with the terms of my motor car insurance Policy (quote number) I beg to notify you that I wish to make a claim.

Briefly, the circumstances are these: Last Saturday morning at 10.15 a.m. I was driving along Caradon Way, Burley, following another car at a distance of about 20 yards, the approximate speed of both vehicles being about 30 m.p.h. It had been raining hard shortly before. Suddenly and quite unexpectedly the car in front pulled up to avoid collision with a cyclist who had come out from a private drive. I braked but unfortunately skidded and collided with the car in front. Happily nobody sustained personal injury, but my front bumper and near front wing were bent and the rear lamp and off-side rear coachwork of the other car also received damage. The number of the other car is UXB 572 and I enclose the card given me by its owner with his name and address. I enclose also my garage man's estimate for the repair of my own car. Will you kindly accept this as formal notice of a claim?

Yours faithfully,
JOHN STRATTON.

No. 141.—Letter to a Member of Parliament

THE LIMES,
HARTFIELD.

(*Date in full*).

John Purdie, Esq., M.C., M.P.,
House of Commons.

DEAR SIR,

As one of your constituents I feel I should bring the following matter to your attention.

Two days ago, on Saturday, May 12th, I went with a small group of friends to the Ship Inn, a table for dinner for our party of eight having been previously booked by me personally, by telephone.

Among our party were two friends from the Sudan, Mr. and Mrs. Luke Banjohn, who are on a visit to this country. When we tried to enter the dining room, the head waiter barred our way and said he had no accommodation for such a large party. I pointed out that a table had been booked. With what I can only describe as a meaning look at Mr. and Mrs. Banjohn, the head waiter said there must have been some mistake; and we had no alternative but to leave and go instead to a popular restaurant run by one of the large chain caterers. Here, I'm glad to say, we encountered no difficulty.

Mr. Banjohn is a respected citizen in his own country and it is appalling to me and to the rest of our party to think that he and his wife could be treated in this way here in Britain. The existence of an unofficial colour bar of this kind must be most damaging to Britain, both within the Commonwealth and in other countries; besides being morally wrong. May I ask you to take the matter up in Parliament to ensure the official condemnation of acts of this kind in future?

Yours faithfully,
JAMES KINGHAM.

No. 142.—Letter to a Local Councillor

57 PARK STREET,
UFFINGTON.

(*Date in full*).

To Councillor Mrs. Beddoes.

DEAR MADAM,

As a local government elector of Park Ward, I write on behalf of a number of residents to air a genuine grievance.

At a recent meeting of the Parent-Teacher association of Uffington Primary School, the headmistress, Miss Fox, stated that it was not her policy to coach the children for the Eleven Plus exam. She gave reasons for this, which may be good in theory; but the fact remains that pupils from this school have for some years done less well in this vital exam than pupils from other local schools where preliminary coaching is given. Uffington Primary School children do not, in fact, get so many grammar school places as youngsters from other schools in the area.

As parents and ratepayers, we feel the council should have a uniform policy in this matter. Either coaching should be given at all schools, or at none, so that all children have an equal chance. I therefore ask you to raise the matter with the Education Committee at the next meeting. If you wish, I shall be pleased to arrange a small informal meeting of local ratepayers who are concerned about this matter, so that we could explain our grievances more fully to you.

Yours sincerely,
JOHN HENNEKEY.

FROM PARENTS, TO AND ABOUT THEIR CHILDREN

No. 143.—Inquiring about a School

"Hill Crest,"
17 Hope Road,
London, S.W.10.
(*Date in full*).

To the Headmaster,
St. George's School.

Dear Sir,

I have the problem of educating my son James, who is now 6 years old. I have discussed the matter with a number of friends and Mrs. Mary Carruthers, who, you will remember, was formerly a teacher at your School before being appointed to her present post as editor of *The Primary School Gazette* recommended your School to me. Would you be kind enough to send me a prospectus of the School and also let me know when it would be convenient for me to call upon you, with a view to entering James as a pupil. Before finally arriving at a decision I would like to see the School for myself and know more about various points which need personal discussion, such as the religious education which is given, outside exams the boys are prepared for, size of classes, and so forth.

I hope you will be able to see me within the next two or three weeks, as I shall be abroad for several weeks thereafter, and I look forward to hearing from you on this matter.

Yours faithfully,
Philip Fitzgibbon.

No. 144.—Requesting for a Pupil to be Excused Lessons

CHERRY TREE COTTAGE,
WOOD LANE,
HATFIELD.

(*Date in full*).

DEAR MR. HANBURY,

Would you be good enough to allow Henry to leave school at 2.30 p.m. tomorrow instead of at the usual end of afternoon school? He has been asked by Messrs. Bateman's, the publishers, to call upon them then, with a view to obtaining a junior post in their editorial department after he leaves school next July.

Yours sincerely,
ANDREW EVANS.

No. 145.—Acknowledging the Award of a Scholarship

26 FRITH STREET,
HASTINGS.

(*Date in full*).

DEAR MR. GREY,

Thank you for your letter telling me of Charle's success in winning a County Scholarship, of which I also received notice from the authorities by the same post.

I need hardly say how pleased I am. It is pleasant to know that the authorities feel Charles is worth help and encouragement in the future. May I take this opportunity of expressing my appreciation of the help yourself and your staff have given to Charles, without which he would not have achieved this success.

Yours sincerely,
THOMAS SINCLAIR.

No. 146.—To a Headmaster, about a Backward Pupil

CLOVE VILLA,
MILTON.

(*Date in full*).

DEAR MR. GREY,

May I trespass upon your time to raise the subject of Edward's studies, mathematics in particular? He has never found this subject easy and is, I fear, rather slow, though careful and conscientious. Now that he is with Mr. Brown for this subject, he seems to be finding things more difficult than ever. I realise that Mr. Brown's teaching methods must obviously be suited to the class as a whole, but Edward tells me that he often is hurried on from one point to the next before he has completely grasped each one. I feel that just a little more explanation from the master, and care to see that each point is understood before passing on, might well make all the difference.

I would much have preferred to discuss the matter personally with you and possibly with Mr. Brown; unfortunately, however, I am unable to visit the school before half-term, by which date valuable time would have been lost. That is my reason for raising the matter now.

Yours faithfully,
JOHN SINCLAIR.

No. 147.—From a Parent regarding his Son's Inattention at School

5 FULTON ROAD,
LONDON, N.10.

(*Date in full*).

DEAR DR. HUTCHINGS,

Thank you for your letter of yesterday; although it naturally caused me great concern I am grateful to you for raising the matter of Michael's behaviour at school.

I have had a serious talk with Michael, pointing out that time ill-spent now cannot be recovered and that he owes it to his teachers as well as his family, to control and discipline himself and to work steadily. I trust you will find an improvement in him from now on.

Yours sincerely,
WILLIAM FITZROY.

No. 148.—From a Father to a Son away at School, Remonstrating

7 CASTLETON ROAD,
ST. ALBANS.
(*Date in full*).

MY DEAR STEPHEN,

I have had a letter from your headmaster in which he tells me that this term he and your other teachers have been very disappointed both in your general conduct and your school work. I realise that you don't find it easy to keep up with all your studies, and perhaps you have got discouraged and think it is not worth bothering. Believe me, nothing could be farther from the truth. It is in facing up to difficulties that true character shows itself. Nobody expects impossibilities and I am not asking for perfection. But I do expect that you will keep trying steadily, both with your school work, and in your conduct. Then, not only will you give satisfaction to your teachers, but school life will be much happier and pleasanter for you yourself.

I ask you to persevere for the rest of this term, so that your report will be a better one than, on present showing, it seems likely to be. Your mother and I send you our love; all we want is for you to develop your abilities to the full, and learn to lead a happy and useful life.

Your affectionate father,
HENRY SINCLAIR.

No. 149.—Requesting a Business Acquaintance to take a Youth into his Office

17 Carpenter Row,
London, S.W.6.
(*Date in full*).

Dear Mr. Wright,

I wish to place my son William in an office where he will get a thorough knowledge of business as it is transacted by people of experience, and as I know of none better than yours, I am writing to ask if you can find him something to do. He is nearly eighteen, strong and healthy, energetic and keen. He had a good report on leaving school, and passed his O Level G.C.E. in five subjects. If you can see your way to admit him as one of your juniors I will regard myself as greatly in your debt.

Yours sincerely,
George Forsyth.

No. 150.—Requesting a Professional Man to Admit a Pupil

Buta Lodge,
New Southgate, N.11.
(*Date in full*).

Dear Mr. Williams,

If you still have a vacancy for a pupil, I shall be glad to place my son Edward under your care as he is desirous of learning civil engineering and I am convinced that this is the direction in which he is most likely to make himself useful. He is now almost nineteen and has passed his A level in mathematics and physics, having been educated at King Edward's School, Oxbridge. His headmaster thinks he has the personal qualifications which would fit him for the profession of civil engineering.

Yours faithfully,
Walter Trench.

SHIPPING AND EXPORT

No. 151.—Giving an Order for Goods

4 Logan Street,
Liverpool.

(*Date in full*).

(*Name and Address of Addressees*).

Dear Sirs,

Please purchase for my account 200 bales fair Oomrawuttee cotton, at the market price, on receipt of this order, and ship by a vessel classed A1 at Lloyds, affecting insurance on the usual basis. For the amount of the invoice I authorize you to draw upon me at six months' sight, and either attach the documents of the shipment to the draft or draw against credits. Kindly advise in due course of the purchase.

Yours faithfully,
William Coats.

(The documents of the shipment are the bills of lading, insurance policy, and, if the draft is sold to a bank, a letter of hypothecation. A bill of lading is a contract issued to a shipper by a firm of transportation agents, listing goods received for transportation, acknowledging receipt of the goods, and promising delivery to the person named. A letter of hypothecation is a claim against property pledged to another as security for debt, without transferring possession or title. Credits are instruments granted by bankers authorizing merchants to draw upon them for a certain sum of money; it being understood that the drafts will be used only in *bona fide* operations.)

No. 152.—Executing the Order

5 BUSH ROW,
LONDON, E.C.4.

(*Date in full*).

(*Name and Address of Addressee*).

DEAR SIR,

We acknowledge with thanks receipt of your order of March 19, instructing us to purchase for your account 200 bales fair Oomrawuttee cotton, and we have pleasure in advising that we have executed the commission at — per candy, which is equivalent to — per lb., free on board. The quality of the staple selected is very good, and we have taken every precaution to secure you against disappointment when the shipment reaches your port. We have engaged freight in the *Dhuleep Singh*, now loading, and we anticipate advising you by next mail of her departure, and forwarding to you the accounts of the shipment.

The tendency of prices in our market is upward, and should advices from your port continue favourable we are confident a considerable advance will take place.

Yours faithfully,
BARLOW BROTHERS.

(It is usual to advise a purchase by wire, in which case a copy of the telegram should be enclosed with the letter of advice.)

No. 153.—Transmitting Accounts of a Shipment

5 BUSH ROW,
LONDON, E.C.4.
(*Date in full*).

(*Name and Address of Addressee*).

DEAR SIR,

Further to our letter of March 30, we beg to advise having shipped for your account 200 bales cotton, per *Dhuleep Singh*, for Liverpool, the invoice of which, amounting to £4,300, we enclose. Against the shipment we have drawn for a like sum at six months' sight, in favour of the National Bank of India, attaching the shipping documents to the draft, which please protect on presentation.

Yours faithfully,
BARLOW BROTHERS.

No. 154.—Requesting Information Regarding a Market

15 HAM STREET,
LONDON, E.C.2.

(*Name and Address of Addressees*).

DEAR SIRS,

We should be grateful if you would advise us regarding the state of the market of Port-au-Prince. We are making this inquiry because of the demand for our products in other markets of the West Indies, and are willing to offer your friends our agency if there is a reasonable prospect of shipping advantageously. Our transactions would not be confined to our own goods, as we would operate in any commodity likely to realize a fair profit.

Yours faithfully,
JONES, FOSTER & CO.

No. 155.—Reporting Favourably

999 FENCHURCH STREET,
LONDON, E.C.3.

(*Name and Address of Addressees*).

DEAR SIRS,

In reply to your letter of June 3, we enclose an extract from our friends' advices, from which you will see that the market is in a very encouraging condition. The out-turn of the hill produce has been much greater than the planters expected, and when this became known a substantial upward movement in European commodities took place. Stocks are low, and shipments inwards are by no means numerous. We are therefore in a position to offer you encouraging assurances should you offer our friends your agency.

Yours faithfully,
ROBERT WALKER & CO.

No. 156.—Reporting Unfavourably

PORT-AU-PRINCE.
(*Date in full*).

(*Name and Address of Addressees*).

DEAR SIRS,

In reply to your letter of June 3, we regret to report that the market of Port-au-Prince is in a very depressed condition, due to the failure of the hill crops and large-scale unemployment. We are well aware of the value of your agency, and perhaps at some future time, when the market has improved, you will allow us to accept your offer. In the meantime please accept our thanks for your proposal.

Yours faithfully,
NOBLE, WALKER & CO.

No. 157.—Consigning Goods for Sale

15 Ham Street,
London, E.C.2.

(*Date in full*).

(*Name and Address of Addressees*).

Dear Sirs,

Messrs. Robert Walker & Company have shown us a copy of their recent advices from Port-au-Prince in which you state that market prospects there are very encouraging. We therefore propose consigning to your care for sale, on our account, a shipment of Chintz, of about 1,500 pieces, and 10 cases of fancy goods, as a trial operation. We hope you will be able to give us a good account of this transaction.

Yours faithfully,
Prince, Foster & Co.

No. 158.—Advising the Dispatch of Goods to Shipping Agents

15 Ham Street,
London, E.C.2.

(*Date in full*).

(*Name and Address of Addressees*).

Dear Sirs,

We have today forwarded to your care, per Carver & Co., 25 packages for shipment, per *Rustam*, to Port-au-Prince, consigned to Messrs. Noble, Walker & Co. Please send bills of lading and statement of shipping charges, etc. to us direct.

Yours faithfully,
(State particulars) Prince, Foster & Co.

No. 159.—Shipping Agents handling Bills of Lading

42 Tollens Street,
Liverpool.

(*Date in full*).

(*Name and Address of Addressees*).

Dear Sirs,

In accordance with your instructions we have shipped on your account 25 packages, per *Rustam*, from Liverpool to Port-au-Prince, the bills of lading for which are enclosed. We also enclose a statement of shipping charges amounting to £23 7s. 6d.

Yours faithfully,
Perkins Brothers.

No. 160.—Ordering Insurance to be Effected

15 Ham Street,
London, E.C.2.

(*Date in full*).

(*Name and Address of Addressee*).

Sir,

Please effect insurance against all risks for £1,500, on 25 packages shipped per *Rustam* from Liverpool to Port-au-Prince, consigned to Messrs. Noble, Walker & Co., on our account.

Particulars of the shipment are given below.

Yours faithfully,
Prince, Foster & Co.

Particulars of Shipment

1/15. 15 cases, 1,500 pieces chintz value £800.
16/25. 10 cases, 800 pieces fancy shirtings value £400.

No. 161.—Effecting Insurance

999 THREADNEEDLE STREET,
LONDON, E.C.2.
(*Date in full*).

(*Name and Address of Addressees*).

SIR,

In accordance with your wishes, I have effected insurance against all risks for £1,500 at—on your account, on 25 packages, per *Rustam* from Liverpool to Port-au-Prince. The policy will be forwarded to you in due course.

Yours faithfully,
JOHN WALLDEN.

No. 162.—Enclosing Draft drawn against Consignment

15 HAM STREET,
LONDON, E.C.2.
(*Date in full*).

Messrs. Robert Walker & Co.,
Fenchurch Street,
London, E.C.3.

DEAR SIRS,

We enclose Bills of Lading for 25 packages cottons, per *Rustam*, consigned to your agents Messrs. Noble, Walker & Co., Port-au-Prince, for sale on our account, and also an invoice for the shipment, amounting to £1,473 15s. As arranged with your representative we have drawn at three months' date for £1,105 6s. 3d., as an advance of three-fourths of the invoice, and now enclose the draft for acceptance, which kindly return to us.

Yours faithfully,
PRINCE, FOSTER & CO.

No. 163.—Enclosing Acceptance

999 FENCHURCH STREET,
LONDON, E.C.3.
(*Date in full*).

(*Name and Address of Addressees*).

DEAR SIRS,

We acknowledge with thanks receipt of your letter of yesterday, enclosing shipping documents per *Rustam* and draft amounting to £1,105 6s. 3d. for our acceptance as advance against shipment. We have pleasure in enclosing these duly honoured. We hope that the result of your venture will be sufficiently encouraging to induce you to ship at regular periods to our friends at Port-au-Prince.

Yours faithfully,
ROBERT WALKER & CO.

No. 164.—Transmitting Account Sales

PORT-AU-PRINCE.
(*Date in full*).

(*Name and Address of Addressees*).

DEAR SIRS,

We have pleasure in forwarding an account sales for 25 packages cotton per *Rustam*, net proceeds £1,780 14s., which we hope you will find correct. We are remitting this sum to our agents, Messrs. Robert Walker & Co., of London, who will render you an account and place the credit balance at your disposal. The result of the shipment has not been so large as we anticipated, owing to a falling off in the demand for piece goods soon after the arrival of the *Rustam*, but prices have not fallen below the level at which they were last season, and we confidently expect they will advance steadily as the up-country produce comes into the market. We prefer, however, to sell when a margin of profit can be obtained, rather than hold over goods in the hope of an advance, and we have dealt with your shipment as we deal with our own purchases.

Yours faithfully,
NOBLE, WALKER & CO.

No. 165.—Rendering an Account Current

999 FENCHURCH STREET,
LONDON, E.C.3.
(*Date in full*).

(*Name and Address of Addressees*).

DEAR SIRS,

Enclosed you will find a copy of account current for your shipment per *Rustam*, showing a balance of £403 9s. in your favour, together with a cheque for that sum. An Acknowledgement in due course will oblige.

Yours faithfully,
ROBERT WALKER & CO.

No. 166.—Reproaching Consignees for Poor Results

99 FORE STREET,
LONDON, E.C.2.
(*Date in full*).

(*Name and Address of Addressees*).

DEAR SIRS,

In acknowledging receipt of your letter of November 20, enclosing an account sales for my shipment per *Matheran*, I regret to say that the result is very disappointing. Relying upon the assurances of your agents on this side that the utmost attention would be paid to my interests,

I selected and shipped only such goods as were perfectly sound and in demand in your market. From your own advices I understood that the shipment was likely to arrive before the up-country buyers had completed their purchases, and that were the *Matheran* to arrive late, the local demand would be sufficient to take off my goods at figures which would leave a profit. In consequence, I expected a result very different from that which your account shows. In the circumstances, therefore, I think an explanation is due to me of the cause which led you to dispose of my goods at what I consider a sacrifice, seeing that the prices obtained were considerably below those reported as ruling in the market at the time the sales were made.

Regretting the necessity of addressing you in this manner,

Yours faithfully,

WILLIAM BLACK.

No. 167.—Explanatory Letter

PORT NATAL.

(*Date in full*).

(*Name and Address of Addressee*).

DEAR SIR,

In reply to your letter of December 2, requiring an explanation as regards the disposal of your shipment per *Matheran*, we can assure you that, had it not been for the absence of our manager at the time your account sales were transmitted, you would have been informed fully on the subject. Until your letter reached us, we were not aware that our assistant in charge had omitted to do this, and we offer our profound apologies for his unpardonable neglect.

Your shipment, we regret to say, arrived damaged partly by mildew and partly by sea-water, as you will gather from the enclosed survey certificate, and we felt bound to dispose of every package immediately by auction, as the best course to adopt in the circumstances. If the mildew was caused by the materials used by the manufacturer in producing the goods, you should claim compensation for loss from him. As regards the packages damaged by sea-water: your insurance policy was effected F.P.A. (free of particular average) and there is no claim on it. To enable you to establish your claims against the manufacturer, we enclose a certified copy of the auction sales and the depositions of several reputable buyers who examined the goods at the sale rooms.

We regret so much the result of the consignment that we have credited your account with £43 4s., the sum charged as commission in the account sales. Trusting you may be successful in obtaining compensation.

Yours faithfully,
BURNS, JONES & SON.

No. 168.—Instructing Agent to pass Goods through the Customs House

28 PRINCE'S STREET,
CLIFTON.

(*Date in full*).

(*Name and Address of Addressee*).

DEAR SIR,

The *Viceroy*, which arrived at your port yesterday from Calcutta, brought four cases to my address. Please pass these through the Customs House and forward them to me by rail at your earliest convenience.

The enclosed invoice shows the nature and value of the contents.

Yours faithfully,
ROBERT HENNIG.

No. 169.—Advice of Goods being Shipped

42 RICHMOND ROAD,
BRISTOL.

(*Date in full*).

(*Name and Address of Addressees*).

DEAR SIRS,

We acknowledge with thanks receipt of your order of April 27, and in accordance with your instructions have shipped on board the *Rob Roy*, for your account and risk, 10 packages as per invoice enclosed.

We hope that the goods will arrive in a sound condition and will give you satisfaction.

Yours faithfully,
CLYDE, HOWE & CO.

No. 170.—Reply to a Letter advising the Arrival of a Shipment

DAVID HOUSE,
EXCHANGE,
GLASGOW.

(*Date in full*).

(*Name and Address of Addressees*).

DEAR SIRS,

I have your letter of February 15, and am happy to hear that the goods per the *Robert Bruce* arrived safely.

I have duly honoured your bill for £200, due on the 10th.

On receipt of the silk per the *Queen of Burmah* I will write again, and will obtain the best price possible.

Yours faithfully,
DAVID STIRLING.

No. 171.—Drawing and Manner of Reimbursement

1,000 TOOLEY STREET,
LONDON, S.E.1.

(*Date in full*).

(*Name and Address of Addressees*).

DEAR SIRS,

We wish to accredit our friends Messrs. Galt & Co. of Stockholm on your good house for the sum of £1,000. It will, however, depend on circumstances whether they will avail themselves of this, but if they do so please confirm it of them. For your reimbursement you may draw on us for the amount at the most favourable rate of exchange obtainable. In view of our former relations, we are sure that you will readily grant us this facility, and we trust it will lead to more extensive business between us.

Yours faithfully,
GLENN, JAMES & CO.

No. 172.—Regarding the above Draft and Confirming a Credit

HAMBURG.

(*Date in full*).

(*Name and Address of Addressees*).

DEAR SIRS,

We have received the enclosed copy letter from our friends, Messrs. Glen, James & Co. of London, with a request to forward it to you and at the same time confirm the credit for £1,000 sterling, which these gentlemen advise to have opened with us in your favour. Your drafts for this amount for account of our mutual friends will be duly protected.

Yours faithfully,
LEO & CO.

No. 173.—Advice of a Draft

STOCKHOLM.

(*Date in full*).

(*Name and Address of Addressees*).

DEAR SIRS,

We have received from Messrs. Leo and Co. of Hamburg a confirmation of the credit you have been kind enough to open with them in our favour, and we wish to advise that we have today drawn on our mutual friends for £850, which we are sure will receive due protection. As our transactions with you have ceased for this year, please place that sum against the net proceeds of our consignment of tallow per *Stockholm*. At the end of three months we shall take the liberty of drawing for the remainder direct on your goodselves, if this is agreeable to you.

Yours faithfully,

GALT & CO.

No. 174.—Executing part of an Order and drawing for the Amount

44 FELLOW STREET,
GLASGOW.

(*Date in full*).

(*Name and Address of Addressees*).

DEAR SIRS,

We refer you to our letter of May 1, advising the execution of part of your order. Unfortunately, owing to the present political crisis in Europe there has been a severe hardening on our prices, and we find it impossible to purchase the remainder. We are pleased that the change which must consequently take place in your market will enable you to profit considerably by this shipment, and induce you to favour us again with your orders.

The invoice amount, £1,462 5s., has been placed to your debit, and our drafts on Hamburg balance this sum. We have today sent the bill of lading to Bremen and the insurance policy to Amsterdam.

Yours faithfully,
GLENTIES, TODD & CO.

No. 175.—Introducing the Captain of a Ship

1,000 FENCHURCH STREET,
LONDON, E.C.3.
(*Date in full*).

(*Name and Address of Addressee*).

DEAR SIR,

This is to introduce to you Captain Jennings of the *Dharwar*, who is about to depart with his ship to Bombay. If you will give Captain Jennings any assistance in your power and help him to obtain a speedy discharge and good return freight, I shall be greatly obliged.

Thanking you in anticipation of your services.

Yours faithfully,
HENRY BLUNT.